Richard E. Nance and
James D. Arthur

Managing Software Quality

A Measurement Framework
for Assesment and Prediction

Springer

Richard E. Nance, BSc, MSc, PhD
Systems Research Center, 562 McBryde Hall, Virginia Polytechnic Institute and
State University, Blacksburg, VA 24061–0251, USA

James D. Arthur, BSc, MA, MSc, PhD
Department of Computer Science, 660 McBryde Hall, Virginia Polytechnic Institute
and State University, Blacksburg, 24061–0106, USA

British Library Cataloguing in Publication Data
Nance Richard E.
   Managing software quality. – (Practitioner series)
   1. Computer software – Evaluation 2. Software maintenance
   3. Software engineering – Quality control 4. Software engineering –
   Management
   I. Title II. Arthur, James D.
   005.1′068
   ISBN 1–85233–393–6

Library of Congress Cataloging-in-Publication Data
Nance Richard E.
   Managing software quality / Richard E. Nance and James D. Arthur.
      p. cm. – (Practitioner series, ISSN 1439–9245)
   Includes bibliographical references and index.
   ISBN 1–85233–393–6 (alk. paper)
   1. Computer software – Quality control. I. Arthur, James D., 1948–
   II. Title.   III. Practitioner series (Springer-Verlag)
   QA76 .76.Q35 N33 2002
   005.1′068′5–dc21   2001049788

Practitioner series ISSN 1439–9245
ISBN 1–85233–393–6 Springer-Verlag London Berlin Heidelberg
A member of BertelsmannSpringer Science+Business Media GmbH
http://www.springer.co.uk

Typeset by Florence Production Ltd., Stoodleigh, Devon
Printed and bound by the Athenæum Press Ltd., Gateshead, Tyne & Wear
34/3830–543210 Printed on acid-free paper SPIN 10784915

Series Editor's Foreword

This is one of the shorter books in the 21 volume Practitioner Book Series, but this is entirely appropriate for a text on the ubiquitous topic of Quality. The book is written in a concise, precise no-nonsense style by two international authors. They are supported in their approach by relevant personal practical experience and by peer-review of other researchers obtained whilst disseminating their research in the academic literature.

The authors base their book around their Objective/Principles/Attributes (OPA) Framework, developed in the first place for assessment and prediction of software quality. After OPA was developed as a procedure for evaluating software development methodologies, it was expanded to include software quality measurement with the inclusion of statistical indicators and a systematic basis for deriving them. The OPA is an holistic approach to software quality and prediction. The approach has been validated through experience gained on a 4-year on-site project, which has also led to improvements to the framework.

Whilst most emerging models and assessment procedures describe where we would like to be in software quality measurement, this book also describes how to get to the desired destination. The authors advocate that the definition and application of software quality measures must be guided by a systematic process that recognises inherent linkages between the software development process and the achievement of software engineering desirables. The authors have identified, from a literature survey and a software engineering perspective, the seven most widely accepted project-level objectives attributable to software quality:

- Adaptability
- Correctness
- Maintainability
- Portability
- Reliability
- Reusability
- Testability

These Seven Objectives become reassuringly obvious if one contemplates the relaxation of any one of them.

Browsers of bookshop shelves can take comfort in the integrity and directness of this book from the following quote by Richard Nance published in a learned journal paper, in which he succinctly expresses his view of my views thus:

"My thanks to the good Dr. Paul for his agitating expressions of these misguided views."

(Page 14 in E.H. Page, A. Buss, P.A. Fishwick, K.J. Healy, R.E. Nance and R.J. Paul (2000) Web-Based Simulation: Revolution or Evolution? *ACM Transactions on Modeling and Computer Simulation*, Vol. 10, No. 1, January, pp. 3–17.)

This book is written compactly but directly, and is short enough to make it a necessary read for all practitioners concerned with software quality – in other words, all practitioners. Non-practitioners have an even greater need to read the book if they wish to understand the practice of managing software quality.

Ray Paul

Preface

Software engineering is a young discipline, lacking the years of idea generation, theoretical development, and empirical evaluation. The concept of software measurement, and in particular the assesment and prediction of *software quality*, is even less mature. A consequence of this immaturity is the lack of consensus on definitions and technical terminology. In developing this book we made a conscious effort to identify and include alternative terms so that the reader might not lose connection to familiar terms and also recognize the variations that are used. For example, "sustainment" is preferred to "maintenance" in some areas. Various documents refer to an organization performing the task as an "In Service Engineering Agent," a "Post-deployment Support Agent," or a "Software Maintenance Provider." We hope that we have succeeded in providing a context that enables unfamiliar terms to be quickly associated with familiar concepts and techniques or readily recognized as truly new uses.

Effective software measurement is grounded in objectives and principles that form a sound, cohesive platform for management support. The Objectives/Principles/Attributes (OPA) Framework for the assessment and prediction of software quality began as a procedure for evaluating software development methodologies in 1985. Expansion of the framework to address the crucial problems of software quality measurement is accomplished with statistical indicators and a systematic basis for deriving them. The realities of organizational needs and limitations are considered in the guidance and directions given. The material presented in this book provides essential information to the individual charged with the establishment and management of a software quality measurement program. Moreover, an appreciation of the need for quantitative assessment and prediction of quality is imparted to the practicing software engineer in simple terms.

Following an explanation of the OPA Framework as an holistic approach to software quality assessment and prediction, the systematic approach to deriving Software Quality Indicators (SQIs) is described. The approach is then illustrated in successive applications to the development or sustainment process, the document artifacts produced and the implementing code.

Guidance is given in the integration of process, document and code indicators to construct an evolving picture of quality useful for project or program managers, software managers and software engineers. Advice is given regarding the interplay of measurement with current issues such as process versus product, reuse, maintenance versus development, and prediction versus assessment. The experience gained in the four-year on-site validation of the framework is imparted throughout. The vision of measurement data as a valuable corporate asset emerges as an overarching issue.

The book addresses issues and concerns in the aggregation of indicator values and includes a discussion of the differences between the assessment and prediction of software quality. The effects of different process models on quality measurement are noted, and some contrasts are drawn between the measurement needs for software developers and software sustainers (supporting or maintenance organizations). The concluding chapter explores the differences in the meanings of the term "quality," and attempts to trace the evolutionary influence of software technology on the key topic: software quality.

Acknowledgements

We are thankful to the several students who contributed to this work in various ways and in different phases over a period of ten years, particularly Gary Bundy, Ashok Dandekar, Edward Dorsey, Ken Landry, Randy Love, Constance Rosson and Todd Stevens. We also appreciate the critical comments and suggestions of David McConnell, James Reagan and Angel Martinez of the Naval Surface Warfare Center – Dahlgren Division and those with whom we worked in the validation project. Special thanks go to Raghu Singh for his technical advice and personal encouragement.

Contents

Motivating Software Quality Measurement

1

Within the software engineering community we are beginning to see the emergence of models and assessment procedures that focus on software quality measurement and the capability of an organization to produce a quality product (Jones, 1990; Humphrey, 1990). While certainly a step in the right direction, these procedures describe where we would *like* to be, but provide little assistance in *how* to get there. The material presented in this book describes not only the destination, i.e. a process supporting software quality assessment and prediction, but a road map outlining how to get there.

The objectives of this book are threefold:

1. to provide guidance to persons within a software development or software support organization who are interested in establishing a measurement program that includes software quality prediction and assessment,

2. to offer guidance to those persons employing software quality measurement for the purpose of increasing the effectiveness and efficiency of their activities, and

3. to share lessons learned during the research and application of software quality measurement, with the hope that improvement can be achieved through a broader recognition of common problems and a deeper understanding of the fundamental issues in designing, implementing and supporting software systems.

1.1 Software Measurement: Why, What, How and When

To set the objectives for software measurement and to focus on the approach taken to achieve these objectives, we pose four crucial questions followed by brief answers.

Why Does an Organization Pursue the Establishment of a Measurement Program?

More specifically, what goals underlie the establishment of a measurement program? The goals touted most often are those of increased productivity, enhanced product quality and an improved development process. An examination of these goals from an organizational perspective reveals their "bottom line" characteristics in terms of an organizational "buy-in" and cost impact. *Increased productivity* is measured on both the individual and group levels, often related to short-term goals focusing on the speedy development of individual software units and usually expressed in terms of staff-hours (or staff-days) and cost savings. The ability to claim *enhanced quality*, however, is often elusive because proposed measures of quality are typically subjective and controversial. Currently no universally accepted scale, standard or procedure exists to either measure or compare/contrast quality. The claim of enhanced quality is often associated with more intermediate- or long-term goals of an organization, and like productivity, quality is expressed in terms of organizational costs, but within time frames measured in months rather than hours or days. An *improved process* more directly reflects an organizational view and is almost always tied to the longer-term goals. Because "pay-off" is only realizable in the long term, e.g. years, the costs associated with improving a development process are not so easily determined.

Based on an examination of the three goals in the paragraph above, one can begin to understand and appreciate why the achievement of one particular goal might be more emphasized than another. In particular, management most often emphasizes increased productivity because the benefits are more quickly realizable. Establishing a continuous process improvement program has lower priority because of the significant "up front" costs and delayed (although substantial) benefits. More importantly, this reasoning suggests why an abundance of measurement programs stressing increased productivity exists relative to programs focusing on enhanced quality and process improvement. Ironically, to achieve a process that consistently produces a quality product, process improvement must be a first priority. Enhanced quality, and to a lesser degree, increased productivity, are the consequences of continuous process improvement.

What Is Software Quality?

The meaning of software quality can vary, depending on a person's (or a group's) perspective. For the software engineer, quality characteristics are often stated in terms of attributes associated with individual software components, e.g. high code cohesion and low coupling among modules. On the other hand, a project manager views product quality as related to the achievement of project-level objectives, e.g. maintainability and reliability. Because software quality must reflect characteristics of the product *as a whole*, and not just components thereof, we maintain that the proper framework for expressing product quality must ultimately accommodate the project manager's perspective, i.e., that associated with project-level objectives. Work by McCall et. al. (1977), identifies an initial set of 13 quality factors and discusses their relationship to product characteristics and measures supporting their assessment (McCall et al., 1977). Based on a survey of current literature and focusing on product development from a software engineering perspective, we have identified the seven (7) most widely accepted project-level objectives attributable to software quality: adaptability, correctness, maintainability, portability, reliability, reusability and testability (Arthur and Nance, 1987). We prefer the term "objective" to factor because each represents a project-level characteristic that is sought.

Notably missing from the above list is any mention of cost, schedule and efficiency. This purposeful omission stems from the *fact* that cost, schedule and efficiency are not objectives of the software engineering process, but *constraints* which are imposed at the systems engineering level. Effectively, cost, schedule and efficiency are "givens" which bound the limits of flexibility afforded to the software developers in producing a quality product. For example, performance requirements might dictate that inter-module communication be implemented through global variables rather than through parameter passing. In achieving maintainability, a system whose modules communicate through parameter passing is certainly preferred to one where inter-module communication relies primarily (or even partially) on the use of global variables.

Clearly, cost, schedule and efficiency can and do impact product quality. For example, if a project is behind schedule, management is more likely to accept developmental "short-cuts" that can adversely impact the quality of a product. Moreover, if meeting the schedule is viewed as a quality criterion, one can easily (and incorrectly) surmise that because a project is on schedule, a quality product is being produced.

How Is Software Quality Measured?

An effective software quality measurement program cannot be developed using semi-related measures combined in an ad hoc, unnatural fashion. To the contrary, measures of quality, and the framework within which they are applied, require a realistic characterization of the software development process. In particular, both the definition and application of software quality measures must be guided by a *systematic* process that recognizes inherent *linkages* between the software development process and the achievement of software engineering desirables. The Objectives/Principles/Attributes (OPA) Framework provides the basis and rationale for such a process (Arthur and Nance, 1990). More specifically the OPA Framework advances the following rationale for software development:

- a set of project-level objectives should be identified from those characterizing software quality,

- to achieve those objectives, certain *principles* are employed that govern the process by which software is created, and

- adherence to a process governed by those principles should result in a process and a product (programs and documentation) that possess attributes considered desirable and beneficial.

In effect, the OPA Framework characterizes the raison d' être for software engineering; that is, it embodies the rationale and justification for software engineering. The objectives represent those desirable claims about the project in total, e.g. the extent to which the product is maintainable and reliable. The software engineering principles, e.g. information hiding and structured programming, stipulated by the development methodology, express how the activities of the development process are performed to achieve the stated project objectives. Quality attributes of the product, like low inter-module coupling and high code cohesion, result from a process governed by the use of specified principles.

Following the rationale induced by the OPA Framework, the identification and synthesis of software quality measures must reflect product properties attesting to the extent to which defined attributes are present in, or absent from, product components. Pairwise linkages (attribute to principle and principle to objective) are then employed to propagate property/attribute measures to the objectives level, resulting in product quality information attuned to project-level objectives.

When Is Software Quality Measured?

To *predict* product quality, measurement must begin early in the software development life-cycle. Typically, measurement begins with the measurement of software requirements. Requirements volatility is a prime candidate for predicting the quality of the final product. Further, additional process-oriented measures are applied throughout the life-cycle phases. Product quality *assessment* entails an examination of the product (code and documentation). Within the classical waterfall life-cycle model (Sommerville, 2001, pp. 5–10), assessment is performed after the coding phase. If the development process follows an incremental model (Sommerville, 2001, pp. 109–110), assessment can be performed on pieces of the product, from which those attendant measurement values can be used to predict the quality of components yet to be developed. Clearly, an instrumented development process is essential to the prediction of software quality.

1.2 Frequent and Hidden Pitfalls

The intent of this section is to outline several of the most common pitfalls encountered in establishing and managing a software quality assesment program. Many of the problems presented reflect a "common sense" approach to software quality assessment. Other noted difficulties are derived from experience. While we do not consider the set to be comprehensive in scope, it does represent many of the more common mistakes.

1. *Starting too big:* Today, knowledgeable software people recognize the need for and utility of a software quality assessment program. Because such programs impact many organizational entities, the committee tasked with establishing a measurement program is often, by necessity, quite large. Many good ideas are advanced, all having sound justification for inclusion. What often emerges from a committee, however, is a formidable design that, realistically, is unmanageable, cost-prohibitive and would take years to implement. Organizations attempting to implement such an ambitious program tend to end up with only an incomplete subset of the identified metrics. More often than not, the measures that are captured are the less critical ones, thus failing to reflect adequately a comprehensive view of software quality. The end result is that users develop a mistrust for the existing measures and a tendency to discount any future endeavors to develop even a scaled-down metrics program.

   When designing a metrics program, start small! Focus the efforts and resources on a specific process element or sub-organization, and achieve success. Use the knowledge gained from this limited effort to expand the measurement program, demonstrating the benefits and successes of the initial efforts.

2. *Collecting too much data:* A natural tendency is to collect data "because it is there", or because it *might* be useful in the future. As stated by Basili and Weiss (1985), such an approach often: (a) leads to volumes of useless data consuming large amounts of disk storage, (b) obscures the real value of essential data elements, and (c) promotes an inadvertent omission in the collection of other important data elements. Moreover, an undesirable ramification of indiscriminate data collection is the error-prone

"massaging" of existing data elements to produce a substitute for a data element that is not collected. Rarely does a retrospective examination of data collected without a clear purpose reveal those crucial insights supporting effective quality assessment and process control.

The Objectives/Principles/Attributes Framework discussed in (Arthur and Nance, 1991) and the Goal/Question/Metric paradigm outlined in (Basili and Rombach, 1988) offer focused approaches to data collection. In particular, both encourage the identification and collection of essential data elements based on a thorough investigation of *what* is to be measured and *why*. That is, first identify the measurement goals or purposes. Use these to derive more concrete characteristics. And finally, determine computational forms and supporting data elements to measure those characteristics.

3. *Supplying the proper level of information for management decision making:* Management exerts influences at different levels. Consequently, software quality reports must be tailored to reflect the concerns at each level. For example, the software engineer focuses on producing program units that are highly cohesive and easily readable. To him or her, reports summarizing quality measures in terms of desirable software engineering attributes on a per unit basis are most helpful. On the other hand, the project manager is concerned with the achievement of project-level objectives such as reliability. Providing the project manager with a report that details unit-level characteristics provides minimal (if any) beneficial insights into behavior which is of direct and immediate concern. Conversely, providing the software engineer voluminous information about the project as a whole does not meet that individual's pressing needs. Accordingly, an effective reporting process is one that supplies information reflecting the proper perspective across *multiple* levels of management. Moreover, that information should be *consistent*, i.e. problems indicated at a high level should be explained by examination of more detailed information.

4. *Misusing information designed for quality measurement:* At the program unit level, error density and person-hours spent to correct defects are prime indicators of the reliability and maintainability of that unit. One might also infer from such information that the software engineer who produces a unit having a high incidence of errors is lacking in the necessary skills to produce a reliable or maintainable product. Such inferences have the appearance of being logically sound, but the appearance is misleading. In the above situation, the software engineer might be reacting to a set of requirements that are constantly changing – producing a quality program is beyond his or her control. Accordingly, one must

recognize that software quality measures are developed with one goal in mind – to measure quality. The use of quality measures for any other purpose, such as judging individual competence, should be strongly discouraged. Such activities paint a negative picture of quality measures and can have a detrimental impact on quality assessment by motivating the reporting of incomplete or invalid data.

5. *Relying too much on a manual process*: Software quality measurement is a time-consuming activity which requires a dedicated commitment by the conducting personnel. Data collection, the most demanding activity associated with quality measurement, can exact an inordinately high cost in terms of personnel time and effort if it is not supported by automation. At its best, data collection (and validation) is still an error-prone, tedious process. Our experiences underscore the absolute necessity of a (semi-)automated process to assist in the data collection process (Arthur and Nance, 1987). In support of such a process, data elements must be defined as objectively as possible, and in a manner that facilitates their automated collection. Moreover, computation of individual metric values, aggregation of these values, and reporting procedures supporting quality analysis should be automated to the greatest extent possible.

6. *Using a single metric to measure quality*: Quality is reflected in a software product through the combination of many distinct characteristics. For example, code cohesion, module coupling and readability all contribute to the project level, software quality objective of maintainability. All too often, however, we hear of quality measurement programs that base their assessment process exclusively on one or two complexity measures. Prevalent among these are Cyclomatic Complexity Measure (McCabe, 1976), Interface Design Metrics (Zage et al., 1995) and the ratio of open to closed software trouble reports. Such metrics reflect aspects of quality, but each focuses on a single facet. For example, McCabe's Cyclomatic Complexity Measure computes the number of unique paths through a module. While an excessive number of paths do indicate potential problems, particularly in test coverage, it reflects only one of the many facets of software quality.

In summary, our experience suggests that the set of software quality measures should be:

- based on a clear statement of realizable measurement goals,

- sufficient in number to provide complementary and contrasting data,

- used to report results that are meaningful and consistent to software engineers, software managers and project managers, and

- automated to the greatest extent possible within the software evolutionary process and recognizing the desirables listed above.

1.3 The Rationale of an Holistic Approach

Today, software development processes and practices are being structured to improve the likelihood of achieving goals and objectives set forth in systems engineering and software engineering. Most approaches include a well-defined sequence of activities that embody requirements definition, design, implementation and unit/integration/system testing. Associated with each of these is a structured process or methodological approach that outlines how one carries out each activity. These activities, structured processes and methodologies have evolved over time and reflect a wealth of experience. Prudence dictates that if these activities, processes and methodologies do represent through lessons learned a better approach to software development, then we should exploit their contributions in the design and implementation of an *effective* software quality assessment program. The rationale described below reflects an holistic approach to software quality assessment, one that capitalizes on the advantages of a structured approach to software development.

Underlying any major software development effort is a set of methods and procedures for applying them during development activities. While some methods may be more explicitly defined than others, the influence of implicit procedures is significant. More formally, these methods and procedures constitute a methodology. The methods and procedures of a software development methodology emphasize and should prioritize project-level software engineering objectives. Examples of such objectives are maintainability, reliability, adaptability and reusability. To achieve such objectives the methodology should identify the proper set of principles to be used in the development process. These process principles also form the basis by which one specifies the environment tools required to support the development process. Adherence to a process governed by these principles results in a product exhibiting desirable and beneficial attributes. In effect, a natural set of *linkages* relate the use of particular principles in the development process to the achievement of individual objectives, and subsequently, to the manifestation of the product attributes.

The above observations reflect the rationale behind the Objectives/ Principles/Attributes (OPA) Framework that serves as a basis for the establishment of an effective software quality assessment program. The OPA

Framework and the underlying rationale succinctly express the guiding motivations that link project to process and process to product. Our approach to software quality assessment, and that outlined in this book, recognizes the utility of those linkages in defining a systematic procedure for evaluating the quality of software. That is, we identify product properties that are *definitively* related to the presence (or absence) of beneficial attributes. These attribute/property pairs (or software quality indicators – SQIs) form the basis for metric definition and measurement application. The results provide evidence attesting to the existence of desirable software engineering attributes in the product. SQI values are propagated through the linkages and aggregated at the principles level to provide a characteristic reflection of the development process. The aggregated values are again propagated along the linkages relating principles to objectives, and further aggregated to form a picture that depicts the extent to which project-level objectives are being achieved. This assessment can be conducted during the development period to predict the quality of the forthcoming product or applied to an existing product to assess the quality attained.

1.4 Background Efforts Contributing to the Book Content

The knowledge and experience conveyed in this book are drawn from two applied research efforts. The first, extending over three years, culminated with the development and application of a procedural approach to evaluating software development methodologies. Refinements of the methodology evaluation procedure have led to a more comprehensive approach to the assessment and prediction of software quality, subsequently subjected to a longitudinal validation effort over a four-year period.

1.4.1 An Evaluation of Software Development Methodologies

The evolution of the OPA Framework and, to lesser extent, experiences that have helped to shape the recommendations outlined in this book have their roots in an effort focusing on the evaluation and comparison of two distinct software development methodologies (Arthur and Nance, 1987). That comparison is based on assessing, from a software engineering perspective, the *adequacy* and *effectiveness* of the development methodologies.

Methodological adequacy is defined as the degree to which a methodology can support the achievement of stated project-level goals and objectives.

Fundamental to gauging adequacy is a clear statement in the methodology outlining: (a) the primary software engineering objectives, and (b) the (process) principles one uses to achieve those objectives. To implement an effective measurement program the identification of expected (product) attributes resulting from the application of such principles would also be necessary. The methodology might state, however, that no measurement program is planned. Consequently, we base an assessment of methodological adequacy on a "top down" comparison relating: (1) how well the methodological objectives correspond to stated project-level goals and objectives, (2) the extent to which the methodology emphasizes those principles linked to the achievement of stated objectives and (3) if identified, the comparison of targeted product attributes, either implied or stated in the assessment of quality and acceptance decisions, to those emphasized by the governing principles (Arthur and Nance, 1990).

In contrast, the effectiveness of a methodology is defined as the degree to which a methodology produces the desired results identified in the objectives stated by the development methodology. Recognizing and employing the relationships described above, i.e. the achievement of objectives through the use of proper development principles and the subsequent realization of desirable attributes in the product, assessing the effectiveness of a methodology begins with a "bottom-up" examination of the *product* (code and documentation) for the presence or absence of desirable attributes. Observing the extent to which attributes are present in the product provides a basis for inferring the use of software engineering principles in the development process. In turn, this information enables one to claim the achievement of stated software engineering objectives.

1.4.2 Software Quality Assessment, Prediction and Validation: A Four-year, On-site Investigation

In October 1990 the Joint Logistics Commanders – Computing Resource Managers (JLC-CRM) began funding a four-year effort that focused on:

1. the refinement of product quality indicators underlying an OPA approach to assessment,

2. the development of automated document and code analyzers to extract pertinent data elements supporting the computation of software quality measures,

3. the identification of a suitable Ada-based software development project by which the OPA approach could be validated,

4. on-site process instrumentation and data collection supporting quality assessment, and

5. a validation study to determine the effectiveness of an OPA approach to software quality assessment and prediction.

Over a four-year period the authors worked closely with project personnel to set up and carry out the validation study. Intentionally, we maintained a low profile to minimize the impact of our presence on the development effort and any perturbation of the resultant statistical study. The effort included attending code walkthroughs and design reviews, meetings with the sponsor, with the developing team and an IV&V team, the identification of critical process activities, process instrumentation, data collection, metric computation and statistical analysis.

1.5 Purpose and Scope of the Book

The intent of this book, as stated earlier, is to provide guidance in the establishment and management of a software quality assessment and prediction process. That guidance is based on lessons learned during the development and refinement of the OPA Framework for quality assessment, and on the knowledge gained from actually implementing an assessment and prediction "program." The material outlined in this book is descriptive as well as prescriptive in nature, and is intended to support the project manager, software manager and software engineer in their efforts to establish and manage a software quality measurement program. The OPA Framework approach described herein is not intended as the "end-all, be-all". However, our firm belief is that the approach described reflects a sound comprehensive basis for establishing a software quality assessment program that demonstrates the best current knowledge.

Chapter 2 of this book presents the OPA Framework and its coupling with the Software Quality Indicator concept to produce a sound, holistic approach to the measurement of software quality. It relates the approach to the goals of prediction and assessment, and notes the influence of the process model on the application. Chapter 3 examines the "theoretical" guidance presented in Chapter 2 in the context of the realities of organizational capabilities, limitations and constraints. Specific guidance is provided in the derivation of Software Quality Indicators, and some cautions are shared from past experience. Chapter 4 explains the application of the measurement program to the activities of development and maintenance, noting the distinctive characteristics of process examination. The important role of the software quality assurance function is addressed. Chapter 5 relates the application of the measurement program to documentation artifacts, noting the particular capabilities and limitations of measuring document quality. Chapter 6 focuses on code assessment as an integral part of quality assessment. Similar to our discussions of process and documentation, we strive to point out both the capabilities and limitations associated with code assessment. In Chapter 7 the challenge of integrating indicator values to produce a complete picture is treated briefly. Chapter 8 attempts to place assessment and prediction in perspective. In particular, it focuses on: (a) the effects of process models on measurement, (b) the differences in using measurement in sustainment (maintenance) or development, and (c) the view and management of measurement data as a corporate asset. Chapter 9 constitutes an in-depth examination of the question: *What is software quality?* In this closing discussion that some readers might prefer to tackle before going any further, the question is treated within the larger issues of the meaning of quality and how differing views influence variations in the approach to assessing and assuring product and process quality.

Foundations for a Comprehensive Approach to Software Quality Assessment

2

The objectives of this chapter are threefold:

1. to motivate the necessity of establishing a software quality assessment program based on fundamental software engineering concepts,

2. to present the OPA Framework with Software Quality Indicators (SQIs) as a sound comprehensive approach to quality measurement, and

3. to relate process and product measures to the goals of prediction and assessment.

2.1 Establishing a *Quality* Focus

To determine the rainfall for any particular day one could periodically measure humidity and temperature for the selected day and then, based on established physical laws, compute how much rain one would have expected to have fallen. Similarly, one might advance conjectures about the quality of a product based on influencing measures like conformance to schedule, productivity, and cost estimates. In both cases, the substitute measures are "somewhat related" to the stated measurement goal, but lack that definitive connection which directly relates the measurement process to the final objective. For example, a more accurate process to measure rainfall is to place a measurement device outside to directly collect and document the amount of rain that actually falls. Moreover substitute measures can often lead to false conclusions. Schedule slippage, for example, can and often does adversely impact product quality. Can one draw the reasonable conclusion then that if a project *is* on schedule, quality is present in the product? The obvious answer is, "No."

In concert with the above observations, we offer the following guidance as preliminary steps to establishing a software quality assessment program:

1. identify *software quality* as the major goal of the underlying measurement process, and

2. define measures that

    *   are objective,
    *   *directly* related to software quality, and
    *   reflect inherent characteristics of the *software engineering* process.

Emphasizing quality measures that reflect characteristics of the software engineering process is of particular importance because it focuses attention on the domain from which such measures are extracted. More specifically from a software engineering perspective, software quality is not about efficiency, scheduling, cost or even functionality. To repeat an earlier assertion, these are *systems* engineering objectives that place *constraints* on the software engineering process, and subsequently, on the achievement of software quality goals. For example, to achieve mandated timing requirements in a real-time decision support system the software engineer might employ the use of global variables for inter-module communication. Although necessary to meet timing constraints, the use of global variables for inter-module communications is detrimental to maintainability. Similar examples can be cited for schedule, cost and functionality. Recognition of the differences between systems and software engineering goals is crucial, and the achievement of specific software engineering objectives is often constrained by the "givens" established at the higher systems engineering level. In turn, such recognition enables one to focus attention on the identification and definition of measures derived from the trends and artifacts of the software engineering process which more accurately reflect product quality.

The remainder of Chapter 2 expands on the guidance provided above by identifying and describing a framework that characterizes the software engineering process, while serving as the focusing agent for measuring software quality. Software quality indicators (SQIs) are also presented. SQIs play an integral role in the definition of quality measures reflecting the presence (or absence) of desirable product attributes. Additionally, we discuss the impact an established (or proposed) process model can have on the identification and definition of quality measures, and finally, distinguish between the measurement goals of assessment and prediction.

2.2 The Objectives/Principles/Attributes (OPA) Framework

The rationale of the Objectives/Principles/Attributes (OPA) Framework (Arthur and Nance, 1990) is briefly described in Chapter 1; more detail is given here. As illustrated in *Fig. 2.1*, the framework enunciates definitive linkages among project-level objectives, software engineering principles, and desirable product attributes, advancing the following rationale for software development:

- a set of *objectives* can be defined that correspond to project-level goals and objectives,

- achieving those objectives requires adherence to certain *principles* that characterize the process by which the product is developed, and

- adherence to a process governed by those principles should result in a product that possesses *attributes* considered to be desirable and beneficial.

Underlying this rationale is a natural set of relations, depicted in *Fig. 2.2*, that link individual objectives to one or more principles, and each principle to one or more attributes. For example, to achieve maintainability one might employ the principle of information hiding in the development process. In turn, employing information hiding will result in a product that exhibits a well-defined interface.

The OPA Framework differs from other structurally similar frameworks, e.g. McCall's Factor/Criteria/Metric (McCall et al., 1977) and Basili's Goal/Question/Metric (Basili and Rombach, 1988), in that all OPA measures are linked to project-level objectives through software engineering *principles* that guide the software development process. Analogically, principles function like a fulcrum, providing the supporting capability reflected in the software attributes to lift the product in attaining the designated objectives. More specifically, principles

- provide the foundational definition of the desired or proper process for developing software, and

- enable one to reason about and identify those activities that contribute to or adversely impact the software development process.

How does one determine if, and to what extent, a product possesses desirable attributes? The answer lies in the observation of product properties, i.e.

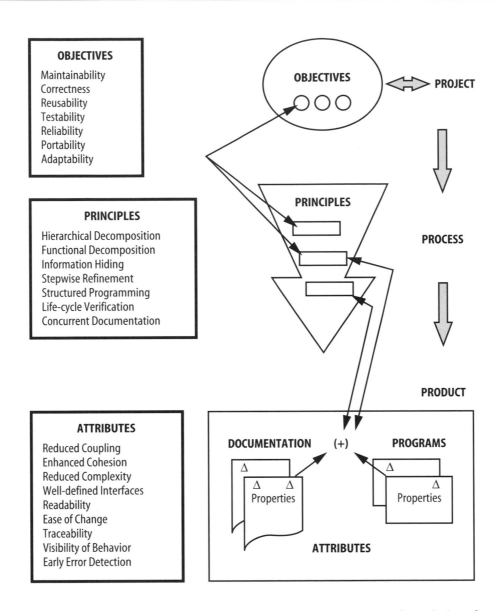

OBJECTIVES

Maintainability
Correctness
Reusability
Testability
Reliability
Portability
Adaptability

PRINCIPLES

Hierarchical Decomposition
Functional Decomposition
Information Hiding
Stepwise Refinement
Structured Programming
Life-cycle Verification
Concurrent Documentation

ATTRIBUTES

Reduced Coupling
Enhanced Cohesion
Reduced Complexity
Well-defined Interfaces
Readability
Ease of Change
Traceability
Visibility of Behavior
Early Error Detection

Figure 2.1 Illustration of the relationship among objectives, principles and attributes in the software

observable characteristics of the product. For example, the use of global variables indicates that a module interface is not well-defined (Dunsmore and Gannon, 1980, p. 149). More specifically, the number of global variables used relative to preferable forms of communications, e.g. parameter passing, indicates the *extent* to which the interface is ill-defined.

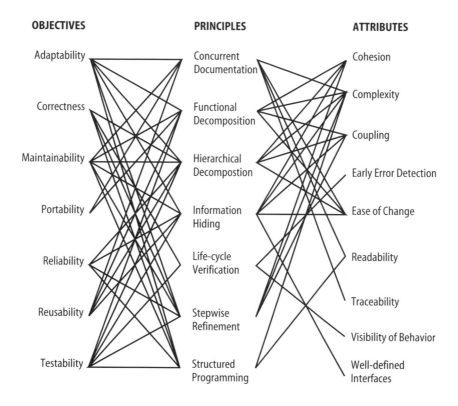

OBJECTIVES   **PRINCIPLES**   **ATTRIBUTES**

Figure 2.2 *Linkages among the objectives, principles and attributes*

Implementing an effective quality measurement program mandates a systematic approach that reflects the best current software engineering practices. We recommend an approach that embraces the OPA Framework as a basis. Through its attribute/property pairs and linkages relating attributes to principles and principles to objectives, the OPA Framework supports a well-defined, *systematic* approach to *examining* product and process quality. The OPA Framework *definitively* links the achievement of software engineering objectives to the use of specific principles, and the use of such principles to the realization of desirable attributes in the product. Subsequently, by observing product properties to determine the extent to which desirable attributes are present in the product, one can determine the extent to which particular principles are governing the development process and, in turn, the extent to which stated software engineering objectives are achieved.

Moreover, guided by an OPA characterization of the software (both the artifacts and the development or sustainment process), one can analyze and examine relationships in the interpretation of quality measures. For example, if one observes a value indicating a low degree of achievement for a software engineering objective (not consistent with expectations), then contributing principles are examined (based on the defined linkages among objectives and principles) for anomalous values. Similarly, the linkages among principles and attributes point to candidate attributes to be examined to identify the contributing source(s). Finally the attribute/property relations enable the identification of the most prominent process or product characteristic(s) influencing the original objective value. The identification of an anomalous value for an attribute/property pair indicates the misuse (or omission) of a critical software engineering principle. The points where this principle is most utilized in the process become the prime candidates for attention. With appropriate reporting one can also determine if the offending product component(s) are isolated or the problem is widespread.

2.3 Software Quality Indicators

The OPA Framework and its enunciated rationale binds measurement and measurement interpretation to a realistic characterization of how software is actually produced. Below, we describe the concept of Software Quality Indicators (SQIs) that reflect an OPA perspective and provide a sound basis on which quality measures are defined.

2.3.1 Establishing a Basis for Measuring the Unmeasurable

"Software quality factors," "software quality metrics" and "software quality indicators" – are all terms used in the conviction that the quality of the software product should be measurable, at least in a relative sense. In a paper by Kearney et. al., (1986) the authors issue a rather compelling criticism of the inadequate basis for measuring software complexity and of the shortcomings of experimental research intended to support complexity metrics. We share the opinions of Kearney and his colleagues, and propose the use of statistical indicators as the basis for scalar determination of product and process characteristics. The motivation for using statistical indicators of software quality stems from the qualified successes in applying them to unmeasurable economic and social concepts. This motivation, as well as extension of the applicable theory to the derivation of software quality indicators, is described below.

Both economic and social indicators are based on the premise that *directly unmeasurable* qualitative conditions can be indirectly assessed by *measurable* quantitative characteristics. The economic indicators of a "good or improving economy" are routinely discussed in business news. Social indicators like "safe streets" are often cited as contributing elements of policy decisions. Meier and Brudney provide an instructive definition for social indicators that serves as the foundation for our definition of software quality indicators (Meier and Brudney, 1981, pp. 95–96):

> An *indicator* is a variable that can be measured directly and is linked to a concept through an operational definition. An *operational definition* is a statement that tells the analyst how a concept will be measured.

Two important characteristics of social indicators are stressed by Carley (1981, p. 2):

- Social indicators are "surrogates" that do not stand by themselves – a social indicator must always be related back to the unmeasurable concept for which it serves as a proxy.

- Social indicators are concerned with information, which is conceptually quantifiable, and must avoid dealing with information, which cannot be expressed on some ordered scale.

The parallels which can be drawn between the concept of social indicators and that of software quality indicators are: (1) both attempt to measure the "directly unmeasurable" through the use of surrogate (or substitute) measures that are directly observable, and (2) an undeniable relationship must exist between the surrogate measure and the concept being measured.

2.3.2 Applying the Social Indicator Concept to Software Quality Measurement

The concept of software quality indicators is a natural extension of the use of statistical indicators in the social sciences. The need arises from the fact that certain characteristics cannot be measured directly and require surrogate measures in order to obtain quantitative assessment (Carmines and Zeller, 1979, pp. 9–11). An example in software is the measurement of cohesion, which cannot take a simple direct form; thus, the need exists to define an indicator that can reflect either desirable (high) or undesirable (low) cohesion in a software component. Multiple indicators can perform confirming and contrasting roles to permit a "hardening" of the softness typically associated with this indirect form of measurement.

Software quality indicators are embodied in the OPA Framework through attribute/property relationships. For example, an intangible attribute of the development process, like early error detection, can be indirectly assessed through measurable properties, like the changing of requirements after the software specification review. For clarification purposes, we note that our use of the term "Software" in "Software Quality Indicators" is not intended to be restrictive, but applicable to both process and product quality indicators.

A *Software Quality Indicator (SQI)* is a variable whose value can be determined through direct analysis of product or process characteristics, and whose evidential relationship to one or more attributes is undeniable (Arthur and Nance, 1987, p. 25).

Crucial in this working definition is that

- the value is *directly* measurable through the analysis of the software development process or products of that process, e.g. programs and documentation, and

- SQIs are *always* attribute/property pairs denoting *undeniable* relationships, and indicative of the *presence* or *absence* of one or more attributes.

Consider, for example, an SQI based on code analysis: coupling through the use of structured data types (CP/SDT). The property in this SQI is the use of structured data types, and the attribute is coupling. One can argue that the use of a structured data type as a parameter argument has a detrimental impact on module coupling. That is, structured data types allow the consolidation of data items perceived to be related in a given context. When passed as a parameter, however, rarely does the calling module access every data item in the structure. Consequently, these extraneous items, from the perspective of the calling module, unnecessarily increase the coupling between the calling and called modules (Troy and Zweben, 1981, p. 115). A candidate measure for this coupling is the ratio of the number of structured data types used as parameters relative to the total number of parameters:

$$\text{Structured Data Types Passed as Parameters/Coupling} = \frac{\text{\# of SDTs in Parameter List}}{|\text{Parameter List}|}$$

where | Parameter List | is the number of parameters in the parameter list (the cardinality function).

Note that: (a) the value is directly measurable, (b) the SQI is an attribute/property pair, (c) the relationship described between the use of structured data types and coupling is undeniable (and intuitive), and (d) the stated SQI can indicate the presence (or absence) of coupling between two modules.

To summarize, we want to measure quality in terms of characteristics set forth in the OPA Framework, i.e., project-level objectives, process principles, and desirable product attributes. Product attributes, although still not directly measurable, are significantly less abstract than process principles and project objectives, and serve as the basis on which software quality indicators are defined. More specifically, we identify process and product properties that: (a) are directly measurable, and (b) undeniably reflect the presence (or absence) of specific process and product attributes. In turn, these measures are propagated along the linkages defined by the OPA Framework, yielding subsequent measures reflecting the proper use of process principles and the achievement of stated software engineering objectives.

Assuming that valid quality indicators can be formed from quantifiable characteristics of the process, code and documentation, then automatic or semi-automatic (human assisted) procedures can be developed to assess software quality (Nance and Arthur, 1994).

2.3.3 Measuring Characteristics of Process and Product

Because software evolution begins with requirements specification activities and continues *throughout* the life of the product (including attendant maintenance activities), SQIs must embrace both process and product measures, and ideally, must admit to at least semi-automatic computation. As illustrated in *Fig. 2.3*, we propose the use of SQIs throughout the product software life-cycle. Initially SQI measures must reflect process characteristics because little, if any, product is available. As development continues and products become more readily available, SQI measures should expand correspondingly to reflect product characteristics. Preliminary work in the SQI domain suggests that process, documentation and code indicators are needed (Arthur et al., 1991, p. 5).

Measuring Quality Through an Accumulation of Evidence

Software quality measurement should not be based on a single measure. If such a measure attempts to incorporate many aspects of quality, it becomes unwieldy and unintuitive (Gaffney and Cruickshank, 1980). If it focuses on a single product or process characteristic, e.g. McCabe's Cyclomatic Complexity Measure, then pertinent information is inappropriately constrained, providing only a limited view of product quality. The SQI determination, embedded within the OPA Framework, however, is predicated on the exploitation of multiple measures, each attesting to the presence or absence of particular

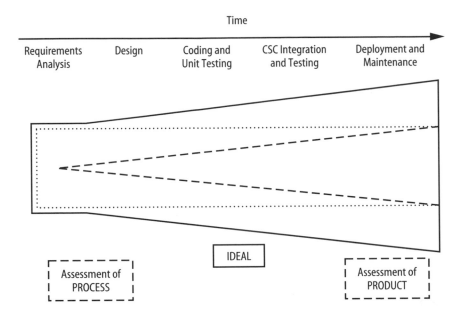

Figure 2.3 Exploiting both process and product indicators

attributes in the product. OPA embraces the philosophy that demonstrating that software possesses a desired attribute (or does not) is not a proof exercise; rather, it resembles an exercise in civil litigation in that evidence is gathered to support both contentions (the presence or absence) and weighed on the scales of comparative judgment (Nance et al., 1986; Nance and Arthur, 1994). As illustrated in *Fig. 2.4*, measures reflecting the absence of an attribute provide values in the -5 to zero range; measures attesting to the presence of a desirable span the range of zero to $+5$. Returning to an earlier example, if we consider the extent to which a product exhibits a well-defined interface, the use of global variables for inter-module communication has a detrimental impact. The use of parameterized calls, on the other hand, supports such a contention. Hence, for any given product attribute the aggregation of multiple confirming and contrasting measures yields one value in the range $(-5, +5)$ indicating the degree to which a desirable attribute is present or absent in the product. Note that values falling in the designated range $(-0.5, 0.5)$ might occur because evidence of both presence and absence is detected or because no evidence is available (which results in a zero).

In effect, the SQI approach offers four substantial advantages over the single metric approach to software quality measurement: (1) multiple measures, (2) measures which confirm or refute the existence of a quality attribute, (3) a relative measurement scale reflecting consistency of judgment and (4) measures

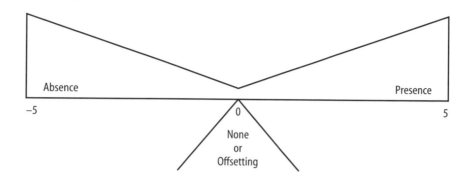

Figure 2.4 Measurement scale

that are simple and intuitive. Sections 3.3 and 3.4 outline systematic procedures for defining and interpreting software quality indicators.

2.4 Influences of the Process Model

Within an established development process, well-defined procedures and guidelines serve as the basis for structured activities supporting product development while emphasizing specific organizational goals. Among organizations such goals usually emphasize similar objectives, i.e., producing a quality product on time and within budget; their development processes, however, often vary in approach and magnitude. For example, one organization's process might employ the conventional waterfall approach, while another might follow an incremental approach guided by critical path analysis. Although the OPA Framework, with the SQI concept embedded, is defined independently of any particular software development methodology, its application must be tempered by the realities of the prevailing process model underlying the development effort. In effect, the process model and attendant activities prescribe artifacts and timing, i.e., the focus of measurement.

Consider, for example, an organization that employs an incremental approach to software development, and desires only to examine code for quality characteristics. One possible approach is to analyze each code unit when it is first placed under configuration management (CM). While such an approach meets its intended objectives, i.e., providing the software engineer and program manager with quality-related information, it constrains the measurement process to focus primarily on code assessment, and correspondingly, on those activities related to placing code under CM.

Clearly, a more inclusive picture of quality could be obtained if assessment includes an examination of the design document before coding begins and a tracking of software trouble reports (STRs) written against the code after it is placed under CM. Nonetheless, practical considerations, such as limited resources and implementation deadlines, often dictate sub-optimal quality assessment procedures. Similarly, particulars of the development process can, and do, define when and where measurement activities are feasible. In effect, tradeoffs must be made to balance the benefits of additional quality assessment (and prediction) with the organizational costs associated with producing and collecting such data.

Crucial to the above observations is that, in establishing a measurement program, one must balance needs with cost and practicality. To do so, one first examines the process model to determine where each necessary data element can be obtained, and then, based on organizational constraints and priorities and on the practicality of being able to collect the requisite data elements, one identifies those data collection points that yield the most "bang for the bucks." Once the appropriate "where, when and what" are determined, the OPA Framework offers an appealing approach to establishment of an effective measurement program. More specific discussion of the effects of the process model on the application of the OPA Framework is given in Chapter 8 (Section 8.1).

2.5 Establishing Measurement Goals: Assessment or Prediction

Within the framework of software quality measurement two complementary concepts exist: *quality assessment* and *quality prediction*. Quality assessment entails an examination of the product for characteristics deemed desirable and beneficial *after* the product is developed. Quality prediction, on the other hand, focuses on the examination of artifacts that enables one to infer, with confidence, the extent (or probability) that a product will possess desirable quality characteristics *before* development is completed.

In establishing a measurement program, an a priori determination of the purpose is necessary: assessment, prediction, or both. Such determination is crucial because process instrumentation can differ depending on the purpose. In particular, assessment requires an examination of the product, while prediction focuses on an examination of process artifacts. Product code and documentation are examples of the former; software development folders and process trends exemplify the latter. Our experience has shown that predictive measurement, while having the greatest potential for controlling quality, is the more difficult and costly of the two to achieve. Predictive measurement requires process artifacts which are the hardest to identify and collect because: (1) they are non-standard and often amorphously defined, and (2) no two development processes are identical, making the direct application of procedures developed by others difficult, awkward and at best only partially effective. Recalling our admonition against trying to do too much (Section 1.2), we suggest that the start of a measurement program adopt assessment as the initial purpose, but with the understanding that *both* assessment and prediction form the ultimate goal.

An OPA Measurement Program **3**

As discussed in Section 2 the OPA and SQI concepts are coupled to provide a structured approach to building an effective software measurement program. Such a program is sufficiently flexible to accommodate the diverse particulars of many prominent development methodologies and the attendant process activities. In this section we examine that "theoretical" guidance in the context of organizational capabilities, limitations and constraints.

3.1 Accommodating the Organizational Process Model

Within a software development organization, an effective quality assessment and prediction program must meet the needs and requirements dictated by two distinctly different organizational components. The first component is represented by staff members who are directly engaged in performing measurement activities. To support their needs the *foundation* on which the quality assessment program is built must: (a) accommodate the identification and definition of necessary and sufficient measurement activities that, with minimal effort, can be integrated into the existing development process, and at the same time (b) provide an overall framework that permits the aggregation of characteristic values into meaningful measures. As described in Sections 2.2 through 2.4, the utilization of the SQI definition within the OPA Framework offers an appealing approach to providing both (a) and (b) above.

The second component is characterized by multiple levels of management, who need to make decisions based on information provided by the assessment program. In particular, within a software development organization the scope and impact of decisions correspond closely with the level of management responsibility. Top-level executives, for example, are responsible for resource allocation, cost containment, and profit margins. They make decisions that affect company viability. While producing a quality product as a whole is certainly one of their goals, they do not, as a rule, concern themselves with which particular quality objective is (or is not) met. On the other hand, the prime responsibility of the project manager is to produce a quality product on time and within budget; the extent to which individual quality objectives are (or are not) being achieved directly impacts that prime responsibility. For example, if a desired reliability level is lacking, additional testing and software rework become necessary, which in turn, extends the estimated completion date. The process by which quality objectives are attained is the responsibility of the software manager. Often in concert with an organizational software management function, the software manager within a project is responsible for the effectiveness of the development environment and the support staff. In effect, each level of management must make decisions based on reports and information that: (a) are *tailored* to reflect the needs of each specific management level and (b) present a *consistent* picture of quality across all management levels. Through its directed attention to software engineering objectives, principles and attributes, and its enunciation of linkages that interrelate them, the OPA Framework provides a basis for producing a consistent picture of product quality across multiple levels of management.

3.2 Measurement Program Responsibilities

The division of responsibilities for software production, technical support, process conformance and product quality must be clearly defined, understood and accepted in establishing and operating a software quality program. Based on our experiences we view those responsibilities as falling into three distinct categories: organizational, project management and software management.

3.2.1 Organizational

Overall, the responsibility for supporting an assessment program is an organizational-wide concern. Support is derived from and based on the desire to evolve toward a more mature software development process that provides the feedback necessary to enhance the development practices during and after major software development efforts. Driving this desire is a fundamental understanding that a better software development process translates into a higher quality product being produced, and subsequently, increased corporate profit.

Recognizing the relationships between systems engineering and software engineering is a first step toward enabling an effective software development

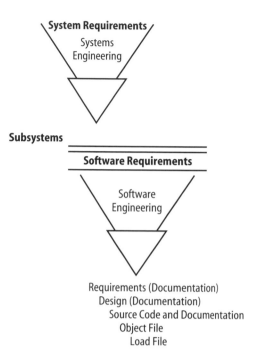

Figure 3.1 The software production task

process. As illustrated in *Fig. 3.1*, a critical aspect of that relationship is that system engineering objectives often form *constraints* on the software engineering process. For example, efficiency goals, which are often erroneously viewed as software engineering objectives, are actually constraints on the software engineering process imposed at the systems engineering level. They are "a given" and must be viewed as one of the several boundaries that the software engineering process cannot compromise. The early work by McCall et. al., illustrates this fact by showing that efficiency has an adverse effect on all quality factors but one (McCall et al., 1977). Other prominent system engineering objectives that constrain the software engineering process relate to cost and schedule.

Within an organization the body that is most responsible for ensuring the production of a quality product is Software Quality Assurance (SQA). In effect, SQA is the "heart and soul" of any measurement program. SQA has the responsibility to monitor development activities, sample product quality, identify problem areas and, when necessary, initiate corrective actions. Although independence is a necessary element, SQA cannot (and should not) act as an isolated organizational unit. They must work closely with project- and program-level managers, and be proactive in identifying problems; yet strive to define solutions through collaborative efforts.

3.2.2 Project Management

From the perspective of software quality the project manager (PM) derives his or her goals from those stated by the organization. The PM is assisted by SQA in the identification and resolution of quality problems. The PM perspective of software quality, however, often differs from that of higher-level management and SQA. In particular, higher-level management and SQA view product quality as a single, all encompassing characteristic. The PM, on the other hand, is concerned with individual elements comprising product quality, e.g. maintainability, reliability, adaptability and so forth. While still high-level concepts, these software engineering objectives provide a more concrete foundation for establishing the extent to which software quality has (or has not) been achieved. Ideally, the PM receives product quality reports reflecting an assessment outlining the extent to which desirable software engineering objectives are being achieved. SQA and/or the software manager produce these reports.

When an unacceptable quality level is noted, the PM confers with both SQA and the software manager to identify: (a) the problem source, and (b) process changes needed to correct the current deficiency and to prevent further such occurrences. The PM then directs the software manager to effect the appropriate changes in the development process. The latitude of a PM to direct changes in the process *for that project* differs widely among organizations. In some cases, concurrence of SQA is required. The responsibility for changes in the software development or sustainment process would require the approval of SQA without question. We believe that the OPA Framework, through its set of linkages relating the achievement of objectives to the use of process principles and the embodiment of attributes in the product, provides a systematic and natural approach to the identification of necessary process changes.

Relative to project management, SQA is (or should be) viewed as an independent entity which plays a supportive role in producing a quality product by providing feedback attesting to both process and product quality. Configuration Management (CM), on the other hand, is a powerful process-oriented tool that is directly controlled by the PM and promotes the attainment of product quality through software version control. In effect, as software units are baselined, they are placed under CM; any subsequent access to or modification of baselined units must follow an established set of guidelines defined by the PM. Such guidelines ensure a managed environment where, when problems do surface, the appropriate personnel are informed, and subsequently, problem resolution is an intentional rather than ad hoc action.

3.2.3 Software Management

SQA and CM provide information which the project manager uses to direct actions focused on producing a quality product. One of the tasks of the software manager is to ensure that those directed actions are carried out in a satisfactory manner. Additionally, the software manager continuously monitors the software development process in an attempt to recognize potential problems and initiate corrective actions before product quality suffers irreparably. To this end, the software manager must have a firm understanding of the methodology being applied and the implications of that methodology relative to: (a) the structure and composition of the development environment, and (b) the expertise and training needs of development personnel.

As emphasized within the OPA approach to software development, the methodology being employed should state its primary objectives: these include maintainability, reliability, correctness and so forth. Linked to those objectives are software development principles that must be employed in the development process to achieve the stated objectives. In turn, these principles form a basis for deriving necessary environment requirements. For example, functional decomposition requires a tool that supports the specification of functional abstractions and their subsequent decomposition and refinement. Based on a comparison among methodological principles and environment tools, the software manager can determine the adequacy of the development environment for supporting the process defined by the methodology within the process model.

Similarly, the methodology, development process and environment tools define expected personnel expertise levels. By comparing a profile of expected expertise levels with the current profile of staffing capabilities, the software manager can: (a) determine if additional personnel training is needed, (b) identify the critical elements that the training effort must address and (c) initiate the training process before those capabilities are needed in the development process.

In effect, the software manager is *process focused*. He/she must have: (a) a fundamental understanding of how the development process is expected to operate, (b) knowledge of personnel expertise, (c) access to process and product quality reports indicating the extent to which quality is (or is not) being achieved and (d) the recognition of how to address and correct problems as they surface. Our experience indicates that viewing software development from an OPA-like perspective provides that necessary insight to realize each of the above qualifications.

3.3 Derivation of Software Quality Indicators

Developing measures of software (code) quality has been a continuous challenge in computer science and software engineering. A literature survey reveals that numerous metrics are suggested for measuring software, most often the characteristic examined is "complexity." Some well documented metrics include Halstead's, *Elements of Software Science* (1977), McCabe's, "Cyclomatic number" (1976) and Henry and Kafura's, "Software structure metrics based on information flow" (1981). A major criticism of many of these metrics is the lack of a "clear specification of what is being measured" (Kearney et al., 1986, p. 1050). Another author notes that software metrics should "empirically and intuitively describe software behavior;" yet this capability is missing from most metrics (Ejiogu, 1987, p. 61). Today, these concerns are even more critical in light of the expanded complexity of currently proposed software systems.

3.3.1 A Systematic Definitional Procedure

A first step in addressing such criticisms, and the eventual evolution toward a controlled software quality assessment process, is recognition that the design of a quality assessment program, and in particular the definition of SQIs, must follow a *systematic* path of development. More specifically that systematic procedure must

- naturally relate the *definition* of quality measures to both product and process characteristics,

- provide *linkages* among multiple measures to support a meaningful aggregation of values and the synthesis of information which is tailored to the management hierarchy, and

- capture the fundamental relationships between indicator measures and product quality to
  - promote an understanding of quality implications at both the technical and managerial levels, and
  - facilitate reasoning about alternative problem solutions.

Our experiences indicate that the formulation of a systematic procedure must be based on a foundation that directly relates product properties and process activities to the achievement of project-level software engineering objectives and to the presence (or absence) of quality attributes induced in the product. The steps outlined below define a systematic procedure for developing a set of quality indicators.

1. *Identify appropriate process/product properties*: Step 1 focuses on the identification of accepted characteristics of the development activity and product properties that influence (contribute to or adversely impact) product quality.

   For example, the use of appropriate indentation within a program is acknowledged as an aid to understanding the program structure and its execution behavior.

2. *Determine the impact of the property:* Step 2 provides a description relating the presence (or absence) of a property to its specific impact on the achievement of quality.

   The use of global variables violates the principle of information hiding, and thereby, because of the potential "ripple effect", unduly complicates any maintenance activity applied to the offending module.

3. *Identify the OPA entity affected:* Step 3 links the identified property to a specific software engineering attribute. That linkage is determined relative to the property's impact on software quality. A positive or negative impact is also determined at this time.

   Clearly, the use of global variables has a detrimental impact on the attribute of well-defined interfaces. More specifically, the use of global variables breaks down a module's interface structure by exposing its communication mechanism to any module that has access to the global communication variable.

   (We note that a single property can be linked to more than one attribute. Consequently, the remaining steps in the definitional process, i.e. Steps 4–7, necessarily differ for each distinct attribute association.)

4. *Provide a rationale for linking the property to the attribute*: Step 4 is most crucial because it provides the justification that *definitively* links each property to a specific attribute. In particular, the justification describes *why* and *how* the property affects the attribute to which it is paired.

   A well-defined interface is one that restricts information access to only designated communication partners. Additionally, a well-defined interface promotes the exchange of only the minimum information necessary to support a module's function. The use of global variables expands the accessibility (and the potential modification) of "restricted" information to any module having "visibility" to that global variable.

5. *Define the measurement approach*: The measurement approach descriptively relates the existence of observable process/product properties to their impact on the identified attribute. Additionally, it provides a justification as to why those particular properties are chosen and outlines how they are to be used in the formulation of a metric.

   To measure the extent to which a well-defined interface is present in a given module, one must examine all possible forms of inter-module communication mechanisms, e.g. parameter passing and the use of global variables, and then formulate a metric that measures the impact of global variables relative to the impact of all other communication forms used.

6. *Define the metric(s)*: Using the measurement approach as a guide, one or more metrics are defined that reflects the impact of the identified property on its related attribute.

   For the use of global variables relative to well-defined interfaces we define the following metric:

   > Let **GVU** be the number of global variables uniquely used for communication purposes, and **PRM** be the number of unique parameters used in procedure calls.

   > For any given module we define the impact of the use of global variables on the existence of well-defined interfaces to be:

   > $$GVM/(PRM + GVU)$$

7. *Define the indicator*: The definition of the indicator is formulated separately from that of the metric to impose the chosen measurement scale.

   By scaling indicator values from -5 to $+5$, we stipulate that -5 denotes a poorly defined interface, 5 represents a well-defined interface, and 0 implies that we cannot pass judgment.

   Because the use of global variables can only have a detrimental impact on well-defined interfaces we define this particular indicator, denoted **WDI : UGV**, to be:

   > $$WDI: UGV = 0 - 5^* (GVU/(PRM + GVU))$$

Although the example used above pertains to the evaluation of code quality, the identical systematic procedure is applied to the definition of documentation and process quality indicators.

3.3.2 Product and Process Differences

Clearly, both process and product measures play important roles in assessing software quality. An examination of each, however, reveals distinctive differences between the two. Those differences are crucial, and must be recognized and exploited in the definition of software quality indicators. From a process perspective, trends and (non-deliverable) process artifacts are excellent sources of information for judging product quality. An example of the former is the characterization of open and closed software trouble reports over time; the use of software development folders to trace requirements and design changes to their manifestation in the code is an example of the latter. The (deliverable) product, on the other hand, can be more directly examined for properties that indicate the existence of desirable attributes. For example, one measure of readability is the complementary use of structured constructs and code indentation. Effectively, distinguishing among process trends, process artifacts, and code and documentation characteristics permits the identification and partitioning of quality characteristics which, in turn, leads to a more focused approach to defining SQIs.

3.3.3 Warnings and Watchwords

The systematic approach to defining SQIs derives its power from a structured process that employs "divide and conquer" strategies that enable one to focus on individual elements of quality while maintaining a project-level perspective. Because such an approach easily generalizes, one must exercise caution when defining the systematic procedure to ensure that inappropriate "quality measures" are not introduced. As emphasized in Section 2.1, productivity, cost and schedule are not elements of software engineering quality. Their inclusion can lead to misinformation and misuse of reported results.

3.4 Interpretation of SQI Results

As outlined above, SQIs are defined through a systematic procedure that assumes the existence of natural linkages relating the use of proper software engineering principles in the development process to the achievement of desirable project-level objectives and to the presence (or absence) of beneficial attributes in the process and product. (Section 2.2 asserts the validity of such an assumption.) Further, assuming an underlying framework like OPA, the SQI measures are computed at the attribute/property level. That is, specific process and product properties are examined, followed by computed measures relating each property to the existence of an attribute. Through established linkages, these measures are aggregated and propagated through the principles to the objectives level.

Interpretation of these computed and aggregated measures can be initiated at any of three distinct levels: at the objectives level, at the principles level, or at the attributes level. For example, suppose that the project manager observes that a particular software engineering objective shows an unexpected low score. Through defined linkages this anomaly can be traced to the ineffective use of specific process principles. Because the effectiveness of a development process relies on the proper use of stated principles, the software manager is informed of the low value and must question whether: (a) there is a deficiency in the development methodology, i.e., not specifying the appropriate principle, (b) the support personnel are inadequately trained in the use of the methodology, or (c) the environment lacks the proper tools to support the development principles enunciated by the methodology. The conclusion as to the source of the low value for a principle does not halt the corrective assistance. A software engineer seeking to rectify the problem can continue the examination by following the principle-to-attribute linkage to determine the ramifications of the problem, e.g. the use of global variables to support inter-module communication. The ability to trace and explain the basis for a score on an objective such as reliability in terms of interface definition at the attribute level *and* to further decompose the defined relationship to reveal properties contributing to the unacceptable value represents a powerful capability for software quality control.

Utilizing the linkages in the other direction, i.e. from attributes through principles to objectives, is also extremely effective because it provides for the propagation of measures that present an inclusive and consistent picture of quality from the technical level of the software engineer (attributes) to the project management level (objectives).

3.5 Decisions and Actions

As evidenced from the above discussions, relying on a model of software development that is consistent with accepted practices, *and* which embraces a definitive approach to reasoning about software quality, paves the way for *informed* decisions and actions that tend to minimize adverse impacts. In particular, an examination of propagated values within a framework that links the process principles to project objectives and to process/product attributes enables one to recognize that a problem is emerging and provides the mechanism to determine where and why such a problem is surfacing.

Additionally, such a framework encourages the investigation of alternative solutions by *directly* linking indicator measures to product quality through *intuitive* arguments. This characteristic invites management and technical personnel to question the "whys" of conventional wisdom and the "what ifs" of proposed changes.

Process Measurement

4

Considering the three components contributing to software quality: process, documentation and code, process is clearly the most challenging and the most resistant to automated measurement. Yet, measurement of process properties is essential to the goal of predictive use in software quality control.

4.1 The Inherent Difficulty of Process Measurement

We use the term "software evolution" to emphasize the fact that major systems are expected to function over long deployment periods and subjected to major functional changes as the systems in which they are embedded change or as new technology influences application improvements. No clear boundary exists between the completion of development and the inception of maintenance (better termed as "life-cycle support"). The software truly must *evolve*; change is an ever-present requirement. The activities necessary to effect successful evolutionary software demand assessment, review and revision following a structured, well-defined and conscientiously executed approach; i.e. a process measurement program. Unfortunately, process activities exhibit a challenge to the measurement of quality which surpasses that inherent in product measurement.

The difficulty of process measurement stems from three sources:

1. the lack of universal acceptance of methodological techniques for software development and maintenance forces the adaptation of measurement procedures to the evolutionary process model in use within the organization,

2. the evaluation of process activities requires an active, concurrent assessment rather than the retrospective analysis often possible with software products, and

3. the tempting use of obvious statistical properties can lead to superficial characterization that is misleading and counter-productive.

As an example of the third difficulty listed above, consider the challenge to extract an indicator of software quality from a design review. A readily apparent statistic is the number of action items generated in the review. However, on more extensive reflection, we might question the true cause for the review of software component *A* producing twice as many action items as reported in the review for software component *B*. Is the quality of *A* markedly less than that of *B* or is the review of *A* more thorough and more revealing (higher quality) than that of *B*? Only by direct observation of both reviews, coupled with comparison with the reviews of other software components and the attention to and disposition of action items, could an answer be given as to the source of the apparent disparity.

A frequent reaction to the difficulty of process measurement is to omit process assessment at the project level, perhaps using something akin to the SEI Capability Maturity Model (Humphrey, 1990) for a high-level organizational picture. This picture provides a snapshot at one point in time of a continuously changing landscape. The outcome is likely to provide little guidance for process improvement at the project level. The Capability Maturity Model (CMM) provides an estimate of organizational potential, but gives little direction for revising and restructuring project-level activities. Recognizing this limitation, a guidebook to process measurement with the intent of recognizing measurement principles and using them for evaluating and controlling the software evolution within an organization is a recent product of the SEI (Florac et al., 1997). Note that while the process assessment in the OPA Framework is restricted to its influence on *product quality* and within a project focus, the evaluation for process improvement in the SEI Guidebook takes an organizational perspective with the primary goal of process improvement.

The CMM *can* serve a useful role in laying out the process model for software evolution within the organization. This model can take a very general form, permitting alternative methodological approaches or can be specific and constraining, dictating a single methodology. However, the process model should be documented, most likely in the organization's *Software Engineering Manual*, and actively used in process auditing and employee training. The Guidebook, probably used by the SQA group, can provide a basis for measurement to improve the software process across an organization, but the investment in such a program requires major management commitments beyond what is entailed in the OPA Framework.

4.2 Indicator Derivation and Distinctions

An advantage of the statistical indicator concept is the ability to employ a number of indicators and to use them for confirming or contrasting purposes. Unfortunately, at this juncture in software engineering, the understanding of the relationships between process activities and quality has yet to reach the level so that this advantage can be fully utilized. We simply do not know enough about the effect of process actions on consequent product (software) quality to suggest numerous measures with any degree of confidence. Our experience has led to the identification of five root sources of product quality imparted from process activities: (1) requirements volatility, (2) use of software development folders, (3) the software quality assurance (SQA) infrastructure, (4) process stability, and (5) testing policies, procedures and performance. In the description of each source below, we follow the systematic definitional procedure presented in Section 3 to explain the resulting process indicator.

4.2.1 Requirements Volatility

One of the few issues finding widespread agreement among those working in software engineering is that requirements definition is an exceedingly difficult task. The degree to which requirements are clearly specified, complete, and measurable determines the success of any software development or maintenance task. A "measurable" requirement is one that admits no uncertainty in the decision as to whether the requirement is met. Every requirement should be measurable, for from the requirements definition comes the test specifications and procedures, by which conformance with requirements can be judged and the decision on product acceptance can be made.

Agreement on the difficulty of requirements definition is accompanied by admission that requirements *will change* during the evolution of the software system. The "freezing" of requirements, remains an unachievable ideal in almost every project; requirements changes are inevitable. However, change must be controlled to avoid the potentially chaotic condition where software testing cannot proceed because test specifications cannot keep pace with requirements changes.

Process measurement of requirements volatility attempts to assess the degree to which requirements changes can reduce the quality of software products. Note that changes can affect software design in ways that increase the dependencies (coupling) among components or reduce the cohesion within a single component. Requirements changes can also produce cancerous effects that worsen unless treated and become increasingly debilitating as detection and treatment are delayed.

Detection of Requirements Defects

Requirements defects are errors in the specifications of software requirements. In an ideal project, where no requirements changes are made following the initial allocation (Software Specification Review (SSR)), any problem traced back to requirements must be caused by a defect; i.e. an error in the statement of the requirement, a missing requirement, or an ambiguity leading to different interpretations. The development process should be structured to expose such defects as early as possible, not permitting defects to propagate beyond requirements specification into the design activities. Defects corrected during the design activities can force re-specification and redesign that introduces the strong potential for loss of quality because decisions are now constrained by prior choices that might not have appeared suitable if considered during the earlier stages.

The OPA attribute affected is *Early Error Detection*, a process characteristic. Reviews, inspections and walkthroughs are intended to reveal the presence of requirements defects, preferably during SSR but hopefully well before such defects are incorporated in a program. The longer defects go undetected, the greater the potential for decisions to be made on misinformation, and consequently, the lower the quality of the developing product.

An indicator reflecting the capability of the software evolution process to support *Early Error Detection* should include both the number of defects and the length of time that each defect has persisted. Of course, some balancing in terms of size is needed; most apparent is the number of requirements. In this case the total of allocated and derived requirements is used.

The formulation of the indicator is straightforward but open to question. As with all process indicators, the principal purpose is to suggest the property desired for measurement, the impact of that property on the process and the rationale and measurement approach. While we present an example, adoption of a specific formulation is left to the user so that process variations, project scheduling effects, and instrumentation capabilities or limitations can be accommodated.

Consider the length of the project to be divided into suitable time periods, indexed by $k = 1, 2, \ldots, T$, where T represents the current value of time at which the computation of the indicator value is being made. Let

Defects$_k$ = The number of requirements defects discovered in period k since SSR

Requirements$_k$ = The number of allocated and derived requirements for the software component in effect by period

F_k = Defects$_k$/Requirements$_k$ and $F_0 \equiv 0$

Then $NF = \sum_{k=0}^{T} F_k \cdot 2^{k-1} \quad T = 1, 2, \ldots$

Early Error Detection: Requirements Defect Detection
= max $[(5 - 10 \cdot NF), -5]$

This formulation of the indicator applies increasing weight as requirements defects are discovered later in the development cycle. This weight is intended to reflect the increasing severity of late discovery, forcing changes in earlier decisions or compromises that detract from the software design.

Re-verification

A second effect stemming from requirements changes is the need to reverify the correctness of design decisions as new decisions must be made. The addition of requirements following System Design Review (SDR) forces the reexamination of prior design decisions from preliminary design to the point in the development or maintenance process where the change is made. The deletion of requirements mandates a similar form of reexamination. Such reexaminations, especially if the changes come in the latter stages, are prone to lack the rigorous attention given during the original activities. The software evolutionary process is challenged to motivate and enforce the same degree of rigor.

Consider also that the detection of errors during re-verification has lost the advantage realized by correction before proceeding further with actions based on incorrect decisions. In some cases the domino effect of the actions based on incomplete or incorrect requirements specifications can cause extensive redesign accompanied by delays and unplanned costs.

Measurement of process capability to minimize re-verification is based on two problem sources: (1) the magnitude of the requirements changes, and (2) the timing of changes. The process should be structured to support recognition of requirements defects either during requirements definition (which is ideal but difficult) or during the stage where the design decisions related to the changed requirements are made. However, the process should also be structured to support reexamination of process decisions from any point where the change is introduced. The example formulation shown below synthesizes both sources.

$$\text{Let } f = \frac{\text{Number of Added, Deleted and Modified Requirements}}{\text{Total Number of Requirements}}$$

$$\text{Early Error Detection : Requirements Volatility} = \max \,[5 - (1+f)^p, - 5]$$

$$\text{with } p = \begin{cases} 0 \text{ if prior to SDR} \\ 1 \text{ if after SDR but prior to SSR} \\ 2 \text{ if after SSR but prior to PDR} \\ 3 \text{ if after PDR but prior to CDR} \\ 4 \text{ if after CDR} \end{cases}$$

Reduction of Cohesion

Requirements changes following the initial allocation can force a grouping of poorly matched software components. Even a single requirement that falls beyond the functional focus can lead to loss of cohesion; i.e. the restricted scope (single function) that promotes the unity of a software component. Functional cohesiveness promotes ease of understanding and simplifies the design and implementation tasks. Even the deletion of a requirement can contribute to a loss of cohesion for a component. Using a database example, the negation of the *modify* requirement in the case where both *read* and *modify* are initially specified can obviate the need for more elaborate locking mechanisms applied to the *read* operations.

The adverse effects of requirements changes, be they additions, deletions or modifications, potentially degrade the functional congruity of a software component. The more prevalent the changes within the process, almost irrespective of stage, the higher the potential for loss of cohesion. Changes that lead to loss of cohesion can prove especially damaging for testing, for test procedures based on original specifications might include deleted sections or inapplicable procedures caused by functional modifications.

Requirements changes exert a negative (inhibiting) effect on the OPA attribute *Cohesion*. Measurement of the degree of the effect should include all three forms of change: addition, deletion and modification. A particular project might choose to weight the forms differently, for example asserting that deletions are not so disruptive on cohesion as additions. Weightings based on the lateness of change might also appear warranted. The formulation employed here includes no weighting based on form or time.

Cohesion : Requirements Volatility $= 5 - 10 \cdot (n + m)/N$

where n = number of added and deleted requirements
m = number of modified requirements
N = number of original requirements $+ m + n$

Addition of Coupling

Requirements decomposition, following either a hierarchical or a functional perspective, are adversely affected by changes. Addition or deletion of requirements can lead to data sharing and communication that couples components beyond the degree necessary in the initial specification. For example, the deletion of the requirement for sonar data to be passed from component A to B might be accomplished by substitution of the source of that data within B without actually altering the message contents sent from A. Consequently, A and B are coupled unnecessarily by the unused sonar data items.

In some cases added requirements can strain the existing design boundaries, forcing an accommodation through linkages that are neither natural nor efficient. Adding computation without requiring new data is rare, but in such instances no increase in coupling occurs. The more typical requirement change imposes additional data, as input or output, and the result is often an added dependency that might have been avoided. A change could lead to the avoidance of an existing dependency, if that requirement had been stated properly or not omitted from the initial requirements specification.

Coupling is the OPA attribute affected by requirements changes that force an expansion in component dependencies or the addition of linkages among existing components. The effects can be broad and subtle, creating a "ripple effect" moving through the software product (code and documentation) like an epidemic. The later the change, the more likely it leads to modifications of early design decisions, forcing changes to be made at higher levels of the decomposition tree that filter down to the lower levels. The process that recognizes the effects of such changes early can avoid compounding the unnecessary coupling through successive branches in the decomposition tree.

The decomposition tree provides the basis for the process indicator computation:

Coupling : Requirements Volatility $= 5 - 10 \cdot r/R$

where r = number of lowest level (leaf) components affected by changes
R = total number of affected components in the decomposition tree beginning with the highest level component affected

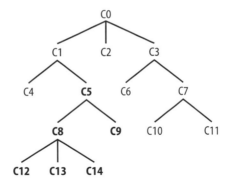

Example: The decomposition tree above shows components experiencing requirements changes in **bold**. The highest level component affected is C5; the total number (R) is 6; and the number at the lowest level (r) is 4.

The value computed for Coupling : Requirements Volatility for this example is −1.67.

Disruption in Traceability

Traceability is the ability to follow the path of a functional capability or a non-functional stipulation from the original requirements specification through successive levels of design to the final implementation in code. Thus traceability is an attribute deemed exceedingly important by the development management and even more important by the life-cycle support agent. Adding or modifying requirements after the initial allocation (e.g. the System Design Review in DOD-STD-2167A) forces changes in design documents and possibly in program design and code that must be enabled and even mandated by the software development process. Such changes often necessitate a back-tracking from the current stage of development to prior stages. A natural tendency is to forego the needed revisions of prior specification documents in the haste to move on with changes. The consequence is often a disruption in the documented path from requirements to their realization in code.

The first requirements baseline is established at the System Design Review (SDR). Allocation of new requirements after this point may lead to incomplete or inaccurate documentation since the tendency is to find the least troubling point to accommodate the added functionality. The deletion of requirements can prove even more disruptive to traceability because the tendency is to drop the requirement at the point where it is no longer applicable. The correct approach, which is to document a requirement deletion at both the inception and termination points, preserving the design steps taken in the intervening period, is likely to be viewed as "needless busy work."

Traceability loss should be weighted by two factors: (1) the significance of the requirements change, and (2) the time period between SDR and the introduction of the change. Both are reflected in the indicator formulation below.

Let s = significance of all requirements changes and the value of s is selected as a real value within the closed interval [0, 2]

then Traceability : Requirements Volatility = max $[5 - s \cdot 2^p, -5]$

$$\text{with } p = \begin{cases} 0 \text{ if prior to SDR} \\ 1 \text{ if after SDR but prior to SSR} \\ 2 \text{ if after SSR but prior to PDR} \\ 3 \text{ if after PDR but prior to CDR} \\ 4 \text{ if after CDR} \end{cases}$$

4.2.2 Software Development Folders (Files)

The use of a software development folder that contains all data related to a software component is a broadly recommended, if not universal, practice. Some organizations have opted for a machine-readable version, referring to it as a "software development file." Actually, the file version can be cumbersome unless *all* data, including notes, correspondence, meeting minutes, instructions, etc., are in machine-readable form. Thus, a loose-leaf binder often serves the folder function. Unfortunately, graphical description, which is progressively preferred, can prove troublesome with a binder or in machine-readable form. Figures or diagrams larger than the standard page size can be accommodated in a fold-out but the result can be bulky. Reduced photocopies can be difficult to read. Machine-readable file versions of figures or diagrams can be difficult to comprehend and to translate if necessary.

An Historical Repository

The presence of a software development folder (SDF) indicates that someone has become convinced of the utility of maintaining a current history of the component's development. To serve well as a documented history, however, the SDF must contain either all data relevant to the project or pointers (references) to where such data can be found. Sections of the SDF typically correspond to the major stages in a development process. Changes in requirements should be described together with the effect incurred in the processing of the change. All significant events, such as design reviews, code walkthroughs, unit test completions, etc., should be included. Project memoranda that affect the component in any way, e.g. schedule, cost or quality, should be included. Project management data that affect the quality of the product should be included, such as schedules, milestone charts, certifications, etc. The compilation of SDFs from multiple projects to form an *organizational quality database*, with access structured to respond to queries concerning quality issues and problems rather than project concerns, is discussed in Section 8.4.

While missing data exemplify the most common deficiencies in the evolutionary process, inaccuracies and inconsistencies can prove the most sinister. A process that includes audits, as well as self-checking, should eliminate these frustrating contributors to poor quality.

Measurement of the use of an SDF "simply" involves the documentation that all data is included, adequately presented, and the document is used effectively. Missing elements, or the failure to recognize the need for an element, reduce the effectiveness of an SDF. If a responsibility of the software quality assurance organization is to audit the SDF, then compliance with that audit requirement (both degree and frequency) needs to be examined. Attention must be given to the critical points of product review and approval, but the measurement focus should be on the process. For example, noting the outcome of a design review in terms of the number of action items generated can reveal something about the quality of the product (a high number could mean that deficiencies in product quality are reflected) or the quality of the process (a low number could be evidence that the review activity is not functioning properly). Of equal importance for measuring the quality of the process is that the resolution of the action items be accomplished as specified and within the stipulated time requirements.

The example given above, i.e. measurement of review outcomes, extends to walkthroughs, inspections, critical reviews, etc. Much of the interest seemingly is attached to the product, but the more important issues surround the process activities and the degree to which they are functioning as specified in the *Software Engineering Manual* or the project *Software Development Plan*. Judgments of the process activities necessitate *involvement*, i.e. the individual must be there at the time extracting the subtle, inexplicit data that cannot be obtained retrospectively which is often possible with product measurement. Subjectivity cannot be avoided in process assessment, both in the determination of the existence of a factor and the degree of its effect. The example used below illustrates this point.

Visibility of Behaviour : Use of Software Development Folders =

$$\max \left[5 - \sum_{j=1}^{9} C_j, -5 \right]$$

with *j* indexing over the values defined in the table below:

j	C_j	Brief Description or equivalent
1	10	No SDF or equivalent
2	1–3	Late creation of the SDF
3	1–3	No log or entry requirement
4	1–3	Missing sub-component data (could apply to COTS or NDI)
5	1–5	Missing phase documentation (e.g. no preliminary design)
6	1–5	Missing test documentation
7	1–5	Missing verification or test results
8	1–3	Missing project management data
9	1–5	SDF contains inaccuracies

An Evolutionary Record

In addition to providing the source of all data related to a software component, the Software Development Folder furnishes the links between the
various evolutionary versions of the software component and between
various sub-components within a single version. The analogy with a
genealogical tree is useful here: the composition of a family in one generation is shown as a horizontal description, but also the relations among
generations are depicted in a vertical representation. The horizontal view of
a software component gives a "picture" at a point in time – a status description, but only when complemented with the vertical view does one have the
knowledge needed to understand the evolution of the component to the
current state.

Traceability is an attribute that is a major concern for both developing and
maintaining (life-cycle support) organizations. While the SDF may contain
all data to reveal the current status of a software component, thus project-
ing a very high degree of currency, it needs to also provide a complete description of the relations among the various generational data items. The data
supplied in the SDF to support traceability can vary depending on the
methodology employed. For example, the estimation of risk and the subsequent effect of the risk computations are key to tracing the development
decisions using rapid prototyping. The logging of significant events, particularly related to sponsor (customer) interaction, can indicate much about the
evolution of a software component irrespective of methodology.

Especially important in the deployment (life-cycle support) phase of a
system is the recording of software measurement values. Tracing the effect
of changes, stemming from functional, corrective or perfective sources,

provides a revealing picture of the effect of maintenance on software quality. The continuation of high quality or significant increases in the quality of deficient components should be a major goal of the Life-cycle Support Agent (LSA), and tracing the effects of changes on quality can be a convincing argument for the value added by the LSA organization.

Because of the differences in methodology, no specific formulation of an indicator is given as an example. In developing an indicator, we suggest a factor scoring similar to that used above. If a prototyping methodology is used, then the capability to explain changes based on customer reactions is important. Risk estimation is also a major contributor to tracing the evolutionary path of a software component. A "waterfall" methodology tends to place traceability data in the results of reviews or inspections. However, communications between sponsor and the developing organization should not be ignored. The scoring should be based on the presence of such data, its completeness, and the documentation of its effect on consequent decisions, particularly changes. Note that ancestral documents, or sources beyond the developing organization in the case of COTS or NDI software, should be included if necessary or at least referenced with an accessible location specified.

4.2.3 Software Quality Assurance Infrastructure

The concern for high quality software should pervade the project activities and persist throughout the duration of development and deployment. To that end, a Software Quality Assurance (SQA) group should strive in concert with, and support of, the project personnel. However, quality should be goal number 1 for *all* involved. Important differences exist between the quality concerns of the SQA group and those of development or maintenance personnel. Such differences are not confined to schedule and budget issues affecting quality. In short, product quality is a primary project goal but is a secondary goal of the SQA group. *Process quality* is, and must be, the primary goal for the SQA group. The proper conduct of process measurement must consider these differences.

The correct organizational location of the SQA group is reporting to a supervisor outside the project management structure and preferably at a level commensurate with the top-level line (project) management in the organization. However, at the working level, the SQA tasks must be supportive of development or maintenance personnel, while assuring the integrity of the process *and* searching for improvements in the process. The measurement activity must be geared to these objectives as well. The quality assurance representative(s) should be viewed by project personnel as belonging to the team. Achieving this view is not only the responsibility of the organizational leadership but also the project leadership. A project manager should perceive compliance with quality standards to be beneficial and convey that attitude openly and readily. Software developers and maintainers should evince concern that the SQA role is discharged properly at all walkthroughs, reviews, inspections, etc.

The major impact of the SQA infrastructure is to enhance the understanding of and appreciation for the process definitional and procedural requirements: the *visibility of behavior.* The indicator formulation shown below exemplifies the various factors lying within the SQA sphere of influence that can enhance this visibility.

Visibility of Behavior : SQA Infrastructure is computed by:

SQA : = .0

loop j: = 1 **to** 10
    SQA: = SQA + Q(j)
endloop
SQA: = SQA −5

with one point added for each of the quality factors defined below that is met:

Q(1): Software quality recognized as responsibility at project level.

Q(2): Software quality recognized as responsibility within the organization.

Q(3): SQA responsibilities, etc. described in the organization's software process documentation (*Software Engineering Manual*, etc.).

Q(4): SQA responsibilities, etc. described in project level documentation with clear identification of any deviations from organizational requirements.

Q(5): A SQA group independent of the project manager exists within the organization.

Q(6): SQA attendance at code walkthroughs, reviews, etc., is required and the requirement is observed.

Q(7): SQA attendance at design walkthroughs, reviews, etc. (both preliminary and detailed) is required and followed.

Q(8): SQA administration (direct) or audit (indirect) of the configuration management function is prescribed in organization or project description of the software development process.

Q(9): SQA approval at one level of review is mandatory before a subsequent review can be scheduled.

Q(10): SQA audit of *Software Development Folders* can occur at any time on request.

4.2.4 Process Stability

An obvious determinant of software quality is the stability of the evolutionary process that creates the products. Process instability, clearly recognized as detrimental during development, can be even more destructive during the life-cycle support phase because the investment of time and training to gain productivity in the maintenance of a software system typically exceeds that required for development productivity by a factor of four. (More needs to be learned concerning an existing system, most likely created by others, than for a system being created.)

Measurement of process stability (or equivalently, instability) is by nature subjective in degree (some assessment of the severity of the effect is required); however, the existence of the source of instability should be devoid of subjectivity. Five potential sources of instability are readily categorized by changes in:

1. personnel responsible for a software component,

2. target hardware platform(s),

3. target language or language translator(s),

4. software environment supporting the effort, and

5. project and organizational management or policy.

This is an area of process measurement where the cause for quality degradation can be attributed directly to persons outside the evolutionary process (those not having responsibility for design or implementation). If the nature of instability is seen as a sensitive issue, we suggest that several persons be polled, perhaps in questionnaire fashion, simply to identify the source(s). While identification of source might be through a "committee decision," we recommend that the degree judgment be made by an individual so as to promote consistency. Having the "committee" provide explanation or justification in their source identification could render the degree judgment more informed.

Instabilities can lead to an inordinate number of errors, making it difficult to detect and remove all of them. Further, an unstable process can undermine the error detection capabilities embodied in the process. The simple formulation of an indicator below allows severity judgments in three weights for each of the five categories above.

$$\text{Early Error Detection : Development Instability} = 5 - \sum_{j=1}^{5} I_j$$

$$\text{where } I_j = \begin{cases} 0 \text{ with no change} \\ 1 \text{ with one change} \\ 2 \text{ with two or more changes} \end{cases}$$

While this formulation of the indicator seems reasonable, or at least defensible, it can be attacked as unreflective of the situation where one type of instability, say that caused by personnel turnover, is so great as to undermine the process quality irrespective of other influences. Thus, this example should be used with caution; it could prove inadequate.

4.2.5 Product Test

Verification, validation and testing are terms associated with assuring the "goodness" of the product. The activities described by each term differ, and understanding the nature of these differences is a prerequisite to effective measurement. Verification applies to assurance of the accurate transformation from one program specification to another: all functions are preserved and the degree of abstraction is sufficient to enable assurance that functional behavior is appropriately described. Validation is the assurance that the product meets the specified functional requirements. Notice that inspections, walkthroughs and reviews are typically associated with verification; testing activities, particularly system acceptance testing, are associated with validation.

While many books have been written about testing principles and techniques, little has been published about measurement of the testing process for assessing the inherent quality. Certainly, the existence of necessary test documentation such as a test model and a test requirements guideline is indicative of an adequate understanding of testing needs. Additionally, an examination of recognized artifacts – a test plan, test specification document, test procedures, and test results – provides some potential for assessment of how well the process is being executed. Integrating the assessment of *testing adequacy* with that of *test effectiveness* is a relatively unexplored topical area.

Although we offer no example of an indicator for measurement of testing quality, we encourage some assessment to be done. Current research in this area seems likely to produce beneficial results.

4.3 Interpretation, Decisions and Actions

Measurement of the quality of the software evolutionary process is acknowledged as difficult in the first paragraph of this section. A first estimate, which in reality is an assessment of process potential, is provided by the SEI Capability Maturity Model (CMM) (Humphrey, 1990). Given the proclivity for requiring a CMM assessment as part of contract competition, a value is likely to be available. However, this is an organizational value that can be affected significantly by factors specific to a given project. The *Software Engineering Manual* (*SEM*), also an organizational document, provides another source of data for process assessment. The process measurement guidebook produced by SEI (Florac et al., 1997) is intended for on-going assessment for management, and improvement and the results of such assessments would be an excellent initial source for project-related insight.

If a *Software Development Plan* (*SDP*) is required (and we believe that one is desirable), then the *SDP* becomes the first project-specific data source. Process assessment based on CMM, SEM, and SDP with no other documents is quite speculative. Clearly, the existence of values from on-going assessments is a valuable resource. However, the absence of such data should not be a cause for despair; the alternatives could help to identify major problems early when corrective action is most easily applied and with the avoidance of late changes. The degree and force of such actions need to be governed by the speculative nature of the data. From this point, project deliverables provide more definitive data for process assessment, and hopefully the confidence in decisions based on such data increases throughout the remainder of the project.

Product Measurement: Documentation

5

Measuring the quality of documentation, while a less formidable problem than the quality of the process, offers a major challenge. Documentation measurement can be approached with varying degrees of syntactic and semantic analysis. The simplest approach is to note whether the document exists, irrespective of its contents. Examination of the contents leads to syntactic considerations: structure, format, correspondence. Semantic analysis in the attempt to understand and exploit meaning, especially using automated techniques, represents an exceedingly difficult problem.

5.1 Motivation and Distinctions

Although the term "software" is often used as a synonym for "program," recognition that documentation is a component as important as code has existed for decades. We consider *software* to include both the executable specification (the *code component,* which includes internal documentation) and the non-executable specifications (the *external documentation*) necessary to generate a product that is both usable and useful. With that view, the assessment of document quality is mandatory for predicting software quality. Internal documentation is assessed in concert with code; for the quality of comment statements, block descriptions, and header information is dependent on relationships with the execution behavior represented. The assessment of external documentation quality must recognize characteristics that are somewhat independent of the executable behavior and frequently far in advance of its specification. This chapter explores the measurement of quality in external documentation.

That the quality of documentation is important needs no justification. Consider the external documents produced and delivered for a major software system: requirements definition, design specifications, test documents, system and user manuals, and the list seems to increase with time. Clearly, the collective number of symbols in external documents exceeds that in executable form by a wide margin. The absence of quality in these components of the system would impose a tremendous burden on both developers and the future sustainers (maintainers). Such a condition could even prove chaotic over time.

The measurement of document quality is motivated also by the need to predict quality at points in the development process which still admit detection and correction of problems. Changing and ambiguous requirements, imprecise design specifications, or incomplete test procedures lead to incorrect, costly and unmaintainable programs. Eliminating problems early reduces the effort and higher cost of removing them later.

5.2 The Characteristics of High Quality in Documentation

The question, "What characterizes high quality in technical documentation?" could be answered simply as anything that promotes achievement of one or more of the seven objectives identified in Chapter 2. However, that answer only begs the question repeated once for each of the seven objectives; e.g. What in a given document promotes the achievement of maintainability (or correctness, reliability, portability, etc.)? Consequently, answers that convey more instructive guidance are needed.

5.2.1 Principles Leading to High Quality

As illustrated in Fig. 5.1 Concurrent Documentation assumes a major role at the principles level. Concurrent Documentation embodies the management of document creation throughout the software evolution so that at any arbitrarily selected point the document set would present a faithful representation of the product status. The principle can be refined into two sub-principles:

- Currency: the updating of documents to assure that changes made during development or maintenance are captured *as they are made*.

- Controlled Augmentation: the exercise of strict control over document modification.

Abstraction plays the second major role in document production. This centrally important principle in its application also takes two subordinate forms:

- Formal Organization: application of a standard or guideline to the production of the document set.

- Reification: the treatment of abstract components as reality in themselves.

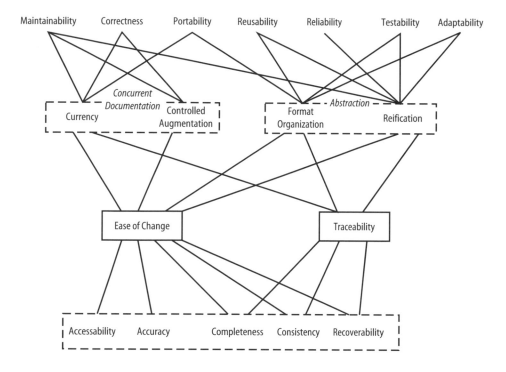

Figure 5.1 *principle and attribute relationships for document quality*

The second sub-principle above, described by Lehman (1993), is relatively unknown as a term, but the application is quite familiar to practicing software engineers. Reviews and inspections of design documents, for example, are purposed toward understanding the behavior of a software system created as specified to detect ambiguities or mistakes that can arise in a subsequent specification.

Following the OPA Framework, employment of the principles above induces attributes desirable in specifications generated in the evolving software product.

5.2.2 Attributes of High Quality Documentation

Among the nine attributes defined in the OPA Framework, three are central in the measurement of document quality: Readability, Ease of Change and Traceability. Readability can be attributed to two characteristics: Recognizability, a physical property, and Comprehensibility, an issue encompassing meaning, representation of meaning and clarity of expression. The former is much simpler to assess than the latter, a claim that is quickly appreciated as Document Quality Indicators (DQIs) are defined.

The physical characteristics of a document include such things as: type and size of font, format, medium, etc. Such characteristics might be classified as message-independent, i.e. unrelated to the meaning in the writing but conveying the ease with which the written message is recognized. In contrast with Recognizability, the Comprehensibility of the document depends on non-physical characteristics, typically associated with style, organization, use of figures and tables, proper grammar and structure, choice of vocabulary, and other features that assist a reader in understanding the message.

Ease of Change and Traceability can be applied jointly and explained more fully with respect to Recoverability. The ability to retrieve data quickly without limitation to sequential search is included in Accessibility. Locational aids such as indices, references, and a table of contents promote this ability. Poor accessibility inhibits the capability for tracing relationships, either within or among documents. Similarly, effecting changes throughout the document set is impeded in the absence of such aids.

Accuracy can be easily confused with Currency. However, the latter reflects the expeditious manner in which changes to documents are made; a change at one specification level should precede consequent changes at other levels by a minimum lag time. The implication of *time* is not present with Accuracy, which embodies either the *correctness* of a value or the *difference magnitude* between two values.

The degree to which *all needed information* is provided embodies the attribute of Completeness. Missing sections, unresolved references and partial descriptions are examples of deficiencies in Completeness. The argument that incompleteness is nearly impossible to detect until post-deployment is frequently heard; however the verification, validation and testing procedures should have this purpose.

Consistency is the invariant use of definitions, concepts and values within and among all members of the document set. As the project matures, Consistency tends to become increasingly more difficult. Controls over software changes through project standards, adherence to a methodology, and configuration management procedures are techniques for minimizing inconsistencies.

Recoverability expresses the capability for reconstructing a specification path. Such a path could be in a generational activity (development or maintenance) but not yet in executable (coded) form, or could exist in varying degrees that support or inhibit traceability and ease of change.

Illustration of the principle and attribute relationships for application of the OPA Framework to documentation is shown in *Fig. 5.1*. Examining this figure, especially in comparison with other published works on documentation, might cause one to ask where "usability" is placed. The usability of documentation is often cited as a primary goal or characteristic. Unfortunately, the preoccupation with usability has reached a point where no consensus on the meaning of the term can be reached. Moreover, we contend that usability must be an attribute, not an objective, and the attributes identified above: accessibility, accuracy, completeness and consistency taken together subsume usability.

5.3 Measurement Approaches

Assessment of document quality is complicated by the inherently subjective nature of some key characteristics, e.g. comprehensibility and completeness. Nevertheless, a program that lacks document measurement cannot hope to support predictive correction prior to code production. We view this purpose as central to the measurement role.

Approaches to the measurement of document quality can take three forms: (1) manual, (2) automatic or (3) combined (hybrid). While no completely automated approach has been published, the acceptance and use of highly structured document standards, beginning with DOD-STD-2167A, enables the feasible application of automated techniques. The automation of document measurement, at least in part, is necessary to extend measurement to the complete document set. Manual techniques must be restricted to samples from the document set; otherwise, the cost is prohibitive. The combined manual and automatic approach is probably the most feasible approach for the near term.

Documentation measurement has three goals: (1) objectivity, although some degree of subjectivity is inevitable, (2) representation, the sample documents should accurately reflect the characteristics of the document set, and (3) efficiency, too costly a procedure is likely to be abandoned. Developing or revising the measurement program component for documentation should proceed with an admission that the result must be a compromise dictated by the relative importance of each of these goals.

5.3.1 A Manual Procedure

A manual procedure where the evaluation is rendered as a single value, such as a real value in the interval from −5 to +5, or one from the set (*poor, fair,*

Table 5.1 Criteria for measurement of document quality suggested by the OPA framework

Attribute in OPA framework	Document attribute	Property examined
Readability	Recognizability	Physical condition of components poor legibility, too small font size)
	Comprehensibility	Ability to convey meaning
Ease of change	Accessibility	Needed documents can be consulted expeditiously
	Accuracy	Minimum lag time between changes at all representation levels
	Completeness	All needed data items and relationships are represented
	Consistency	Invariant use of all definitions, concepts, etc.
Traceability	Recoverability	Capability to reconstruct a specific path

good, excellent), can provide some recognition of potential problem spots when used to compare document components. However, the procedure is not very helpful in suggesting how improvements can be realized. If a manual procedure is employed, then the identification of explicit criteria on which document quality is judged is preferable to the single-value labeling. The criteria suggested by the OPA Framework are described above and summarized in Table 5.1. For each criterion (document property), an indicator should be defined that can be employed in a human examination. Examples are given in Table 5.2.

The examiner should review the selected documents with a checksheet, recording a score for each indicator. (Note that a Document Quality Indicator (DQI) is an attribute/property pair in conformance with the definition given in Section 2.) Use of or conversion to the −5 to +5 scale of measurement is necessary if the attribute values are to be propagated upward to form principle and objective computations.

5.3.2 An Automated Procedure

The DOCALYZER document quality analyzer demonstrates an automated application to a subset of the properties created in the seminal study. The application of DOCALYZER requires that: (1) the documentation deliveries conform to a structured standard and (2) the standard be described to DOCALYZER in a formal manner. While only 11 of the 32 proposed DQI's could be automated, and only ten prove usable, the ability of that subset to match the assessment of expert assessors is demonstrated, giving encouragement

Table 5.2 Examples of documentation quality indicators (DQIs) (DQI = document attribute/ document property pair)

Document attribute	Document property	Property measurement
Accessibility	Completeness of table of contents (TOC)	Degree to which all important topics are contained in TOC
Accuracy	Code utilization	Degree to which existing code components are necessary to fulfill design specifications
Completeness	Documentation	Degree to which software components required by standard or project guidelines are present
Comprehensibility	Format appropriateness	Suitability of presentation style or layout (use of charts, graphs, tables)
Consistency	Invariance of concept	Extent to which the meaning of each requirement is preserved through all specifications to date
Recognizability	Adequacy of print	Degree to which physical display techniques reflect knowledge of human needs and limitations
Recoverability	Reverse path reconstruction	Extent to which claimed functionality of software component can be substantiated in prior specifications

to the prospect for totally automated analysis (Dorsey 1992). Table 5.3 shows the 11 indicators included in DOCALYZER to give an indication of the extent to which automated analysis can be employed.

The ability to automate indicators related to specific attributes more than others is apparent in Table 5.3, where seven of the 11 pertain to Accessibility. The rather "mechanical" nature of Accessibility makes it more amenable to automated analysis than Recognizability for example. A deficiency of the current DOCALYZER prototype – no analysis of inter-document properties – must be removed to address Consistency and Recoverability in a satisfactory fashion.

The approach taken in DOCALYZER is statistical in nature. Frequency counts form the values of selected indicators. An alternative approach that could be followed is to build an *expert system* that would apply automatically the criteria characterizing document quality in the opinion of a human documentation specialist. One caution here is that the predictive purpose of document quality assessment mandates that the expert's judgment be validated; i.e. the expert demonstrate the ability to recognize documentation characteristics that do affect software quality based on post-deployment results.

Table 5.3 Document quality indicators automated in DOCALYZE

Document attribute	Document property	Property measurement
Accessibility	Locational accuracy of index	Accuracy with which index cites location of terms
	Order of glossary	Use of alphabetical ordering format
	Glossary completeness	Degree to which necessary terms are contained in the glossary
	Appropriateness of references	Proportion of proper (needed) references
	Correctness of table of contents (TOC)	Accuracy of section titles appearing in TOC
	Locational accuracy of TOC	Accuracy of TOC in citing locations and titles
	Completeness of TOC	Degree to which important topics contained in documentation are included in TOC
Completeness	Missing/incorrect references	Proportion of missing references
	To be defined/to be specified frequency	Frequency of TBD/TBS use within the document
Comprehensibility	Acronym usage	Degree to which acronym use is well-defined and consistent
	Keyword context consistency	Degree to which key words are used consistently throughout a document set

5.3.3 A Combined Approach

Progressing to fully automated analysis of document quality should be a goal; but the hurdles to achieving this goal are not insignificant. We advise a strategy framed within practical limitations:

- Identify from the literature, or define based on experience, those document characteristics which capture quality as your organization understands and values it.

- Following the systematic procedure outlined in Section 3.3, construct Document Quality Indicators for those characteristics which admit definition. (Do not force entries in the definitional template; the current understanding of some characteristics is not sufficient for a DQI definition.)

- For each DQI, assess the importance of the indicator in conveying the quality of the document (high, moderate, low) and estimate the effort (time and/or dollars) to achieve automated application (high, moderate, low).

- Examining the value pair (importance, effort) for each DQI, consider first those with (high, high) for inclusion in the manual procedure. Follow with those with (high, moderate), then (high, low), adding indicators for manual use when possible.

- Consider the resulting set of DQIs in the manual procedure. If the set is felt sufficient for quality prediction, then establish the set as the standard or base. If the set is too large, reduce the set by deleting DQIs with value pair (high, low), followed by (high, moderate), then (high, high) if necessary. If too few indicators comprise the set, then repeat the examination above, beginning with the (moderate, high) values and progressing downward in effort.

The intent of the above strategy is to develop a manual procedure, which will require training to apply, while at the same time laying out a plan for progressive automation of the DQI measurement. Thus, having completed the set of DQIs following the manual, the excluded indicators should be reviewed to develop a schedule for automating those deemed necessary. The basis for selecting DQIs in the above strategy should assure that members of the manual set, if candidates for automation, are among the last. The strategy preserves a stable manual procedure for as long as possible.

5.4 Interpretation, Decisions and Actions

The interpretation of DQI values, especially in their integration with the values of process indicators, is highly dependent on the maturity of the organization, and in particular, in its history with software measurement. Limiting the discussion to document quality, an initial exercise should be to identify those problems which appear to be most prevalent in causing low or unacceptable DQI values. Corrective fixes are then developed for these problems, including example excerpts reflecting the absence and presence of the attribute. This instructive material should be included in a specific chapter of the *Software Engineering Manual* devoted to document design, generation and review. If the writing problems are particularly widespread, this chapter or an expanded version could be created as a separate pamphlet, readily accessible during process activities in which documentation is created.

5.4.1 Beginning a Document Quality Measurement Program

Document quality measurement, if preceded by process measurement, initiates with the first qualified deliverable (likely to be the requirements document) and begins the transition to product-oriented assessment augmenting the process measurement. Some variation in values for process and document indicators should be expected, especially with a new measurement program. Such variation could cause the conclusion that the two are measuring quality in very different ways. Despite expecting some variation, an examination of the process and the products delivered to that time is in order. Potential problems (effects) seen in indicator values are listed along with the possible causes in Table 5.4. The suggested order of check is simply a guess based on which causes seem more likely, lacking any project-specific information.

A distinct advantage of the use of Software Quality Indicators within the OPA Framework is the potential for confirming information gained through the application of multiple indicators. When indicator values, grouped in pairs or triples, do not relate to support an interpretation, then the measurement procedure should be examined to assess the cause of the unexpected results. That our intuition is sometimes faulty should be acknowledged, but assurance that such is the case is a recognized responsibility.

5.4.2 Integrating Process and Document Measurement

Augmenting the information provided by Process Indicators with DQI results gives a much stronger basis for decisions regarding the quality prediction. Software components with notably lower values need to be examined closely. As the document products continue to be generated the information support becomes increasingly stronger. Decisions on inspection schedules should consider the information rendered by the SQIs; re-inspections may be warranted if low quality persists. Regressive inspections, i.e. inspection of previously inspected specifications to include corrections and improvements, should be mandatory actions. If software quality measurement is to derive the maximum benefit for the project, then the predictive capability of both process and document indicators must be employed in the decisions made.

That differences exist among software-intensive projects is undeniable. The choice of methodology for software evolution can lead to differences. Yet, those differences may exert little influence on software quality because of

Table 5.4 Checklist for diagnosing possible problems with document quality measurement

Problems (effects with SQIs)	Suggested order of check	Potential cause of problems (effects)
1. Large variations in a single indicator over the set of software components	a, b, c	(a) Different experience levels among component creators
		(b) Varying knowledge of methodology
2. Large variations among Process Indicators for single software component	b, d, a	(c) Differing experience levels with environment tools (utilities) among component creators
		(d) Inadequate training for some personnel
3. Document Quality Indicators score much higher than Process Indicators	f, g, e	(e) Process quality may not be reflected adequately by Process Indicators
4. Document Quality Indicators score much lower than Process Indicators	c, e, d	(f) DQI values appear to inflated by low denominator values (component size, typically)
		(g) Process Indicator may not apply because of methodology or project guidelines
5. Indicators appear to cluster in the interval (0.4, 0.6)	g, h	(h) Natural tendency is for SQIs to cluster near "0"

the approach taken by the OPA Framework. Functional influences are minimized; the focus is where it should be: *the engineering of high quality software.* Consequently, we believe in maintaining project measurement histories that promote the comparison of current values with past results. The key consideration for inter-project comparison of measures is to avoid the cases where other factors render the comparisons meaningless. Comparisons of indicator values within a project are obviously a plus, but comparisons between projects, with some attention to avoiding the "poor mixes," can be extremely informative. The project measurement history for software quality, i.e. the quality database described in Section 8.4, should be regarded as a corporate asset, and used in the planning and management of subsequent projects.

Product Measurement: Code 6

Developing measures of software (code) quality has been a long-term challenge in computer science and software engineering. A survey of articles in the literature reveals that many metrics are available for measuring software. Some well documented metrics include Halstead's *Elements of Software Science* (1977), McCabe's Cyclomatic Number (1976) and Henry and Kafura's *"Software structure metrics based on information flow"* (1981). A major criticism of using any one of these metrics in isolation is that it provides a snapshot of only one particular aspect of code quality. For example, McCabe's Cyclomatic Complexity reports the number of paths through a program. While this particular characteristic is certainly related to program quality, it says nothing about the many other contributors to code quality, e.g. intermodule coupling, the use of structured programming constructs, code commenting, and so forth. Even if one employs a collection of existing metrics, each developed in relative isolation and narrowly focused on particular characteristics, drawing a conclusion from disparate measures is indeed difficult.

The objective of this chapter is to outline and explain one process for identifying and defining measures of code quality. In the following subsection a systematic procedure for deriving measures based on quality attributes is presented. This procedure outlines a process for: (1) identifying language structures supporting the development of code which exhibits quality characteristics, and (2) formulating measures that reflect the intended benefits of including such structures in the language. Section 6.2 presents an overview of what are considered to be the attributes of code quality. The outline includes the description of an abbreviated, yet structured, indicator derivation for each attribute. Finally, the last subsection presents a discussion that focuses on the distinctive capabilities and limitations in measuring code quality.

6.1 Indicator Distinction and Derivation

Section 3.3.1 introduces a systematic procedure for defining software quality that is applicable to the definition of process, documentation and code quality indicators. The following set of steps are intended to focus that process on the definition of code quality indicators, and in particular, as they relate to the specified implementation language. More specifically, the first three steps outline how one uses a language definition and rationale to identify potential structures supporting software quality engineering. Steps 4 and 5 extend that process by describing how to factor in the usage of identified language structures and how that usage translates into the formulation of measures and metrics. In total, the five steps outlined below justify, strengthen and further substantiate the utility of quality indicators based on definitive relationships between software engineering attributes and observable properties of the code. Although we describe the procedure for Ada, the steps are easily generalized to accommodate any structured, imperative language.

Step 1: Identifying, Categorizing and Classifying Crucial Language Components

The initial task in defining a procedure for assessing the quality of a language product is to:

- identify those language components deemed necessary and crucial to the quality assessment process, and then

- formulate a categorization scheme that permits language components to be examined at both the individual and aggregated levels.

In concert with this approach, the categorization scheme we used initially employs a partitioning criteria proposed by Ghezzi and Jazayeri (1982) and Wichmann (1984b); that is, the partitioning of language components along aggregate structures designed to support distinct capabilities. To assist in the partitioning of procedural languages, we view those capabilities in terms of program construction. In particular, procedurally-based programs most commonly posses three aggregate structures: data types, statement level control structures and unit level control structures. By selecting a specific language, e.g. Ada, we can further decompose the partitioning as follows:

- Data Types
    - Strings
    - Records and Record Descriminants
    - Arrays
- Statement Level Control Structures

- Conditional Statements
- Looping Constructs
  * For, while, named loops, iterators
  * Exit statements
- Block Structures
- Assignment Statements
- Procedure and Function Invocation Statements
● Unit Level Control Structures
  - Subprograms
    * Default Parameters, Name Overloading, Parameter Passing
  - Packages
    * Specification
    * Body
  - Generics
  - Tasking
    * Concurrency Specification
  - Exception Handling

The above categorization is not intended to cover all Ada-specific language components, but assist in decomposing a language definition into manageable, well-understood components that play a prominent role in the engineering of a quality product, and hence, a potential artifact for measurement. Bundy (1990) offers a more detailed explanation of identifying, categorizing, and classifying Ada language constructs with respect to software quality assessment within the OPA Framework.

Step 2: Understanding the Rationale for Component Inclusion

Before employing code analysis as part of a software quality procedure, one must *acquire a firm understanding of why particular language constructs have been included in a language definition.* In some cases, the rationale might simply be that a specific capability is needed, e.g. looping. From the perspectives of software engineering and software quality assessment, however, the rationale for including constructs like user defined types, packages, and block structures is particularly important, especially when they are purported to support desirable product design and development capabilities. That rationale is often found in publications describing research results, development efforts and language design criteria/issues. For example, the designers of Ada have provided the publication: *Rationale for the Design of the Ada Programming Language* (ADAR95). Using the Ada "package" as a representative example, the next paragraph outlines the type of information used in synthesizing an adequate understanding for including particular language elements in the definition of Ada.

According to (ADAR95) packages are one mechanism through which the programmer can group constants, type declarations, variables, and/or subprograms. The intent is that the programmer uses packages to group related items. From a software engineering perspective, this particular use of packages is appealing because it promotes code cohesion (Ross, 1986). Packages are also a powerful tool in supporting the specification of abstractions. The ability to localize implementation details and to group related collections of information are a prerequisite for defining abstract data types in a language. Again, from a software engineering perspective, the capability to specify abstract data types and to force the use of predefined operations to modify data structures promotes a well-defined interface, functional cohesion, and reduced complexity.

Step 3: Assessing Component Importance from a Software Engineering Perspective

To exploit the OPA Framework one must determine each individual component's contribution to the achievement of desirable software engineering objectives, its support in the use of accepted software engineering principles, and/or its ability to induce desirable software engineering attributes in the resulting product. Important in the OPA Framework is the impact of a component on product quality – it can be beneficial or detrimental. For example, operator overloading generally enhances program readability (Wichmann, 1984a, Ghezzi and Jazayeri, 1982). If used indiscriminately, however, it can have the opposite effect (Ghezzi and Jazayeri, 1982).

From a language standpoint, the literature abounds with citations attesting to the "software engineering goodness" of several language constructs. Continuing with Ada packages as our example, because they support the definition of multiple types of abstractions, e.g. named collections of declarations, subroutine libraries, abstract state machines, and abstract data types, packages are deemed extremely important in achieving a high quality software product. More specifically, abstract data types are fundamental to supporting the software engineering principle of information hiding (ADAR95). That is, packages defining abstract data types provide the type declaration for an abstract data type and methods for manipulating the data type. What is hidden from the user is the sequence of coded instructions supporting the manipulative operations. Also, the user is forced to modify the abstract data type through the specified operations. This form of information hiding is particularly beneficial when maintenance is required because it tends to minimize the "ripple effect" that change can have. As also discussed by Booch (1983, 1987), packages are crucial in supporting modularity, localization, reusability, and portability, all of which are highly supportive of software engineering objectives.

Step 4: Identifying the Impact of Component Usage on Desirable Software Engineering Attributes

In the third step described above language components are associated with rather high-level software engineering characteristics such as maintainability, reliability, information hiding, and modularity. The fourth step is to *identify: (a) how each language construct can be used (or misused) during software development, (b) which product attributes are affected, and (c) how they are affected.* Within the OPA Framework the fourth step is crucial because it relates the use of each language construct to the impact it has on one or more of the (less abstract) software engineering attributes. This fourth step is illustrated below by considering the impact of packages relative to selected software engineering attributes.

As a basis, we examine the four proposed uses of packages in linking package properties to software engineering attributes. For example, packages that contain only type declarations indicate code cohesion (Ross, 1986). The other three proposed uses are packages to define abstract data types, packages to define abstract state machines and packages to define subprogram units. Although all four of these uses induce desirable attributes in the developed product (see (Gannon et al., 1986; Embley and Woodfield, 1988; Booch, 1987), respectively), the improper use of packages can also have a negative impact on the desirable product attributes. For example, the use of packages to group type declarations has diminishing returns when too many type declarations are exported. This misuse hinders ease of change because program units must be unnecessarily checked for possible impacts caused by changes to declaration packages.

Consider as a detailed illustration of the above, the use of packages to define abstract data types (we refer to such packages at ADT packages). The benefits (relative to the inducement of desirable software engineering attributes) of ADT packages are enhanced cohesion (functional and logical), a well-defined interface via the ADT, and enhanced ease of change for program units importing (or "withing") the ADT package. The improved cohesion results from the grouping of the ADT declarations and access operations within one package. A well-defined ADT interface is achieved by using the package specification to house the subprogram specification for each ADT and then using private or limited private types to restrict access to the ADT. From a different perspective, because of the capabilities provided by packages, the use of ADTs has additional beneficial effects in terms of reduced code complexity and improved readability. Without further elaboration, it suffices to say that the definition of ADTs through packages embraces the use of abstractions that hide superfluous details from the ADT user.

Step 5: Identifying Properties, Defining Indicators, and Formulating Measures and Metrics

The fourth step of the metric development procedure describes the impact that component uses and abuses have on the software engineering attributes. In Step 5 we identify and formally link product properties (language elements) to those software engineering attributes. Building on that attribute/property relationship, we then define a measurement approach, supporting metric(s) and finally the indicator. These activities are considered as a single step in the derivation of code indicators because they are so intrinsically related. To illustrate Step 5 of the development procedure, the remainder of this section focuses on the identification of properties indicative of the presence of the attribute cohesion relative to the use of packages in defining groups of subprograms.

With attention focused on a single attribute, the process begins with the identification of properties that indicate the presence or absence of that attribute. In the cohesion example, the task is to identify characteristics that a *cohesive* package would exhibit. One such characteristic is the extent to which subprograms defined within a package are utilized. In particular, each program unit that "withs" the package of subprograms utilizes a percentage of the subprograms. A very low utilization suggests that the subprograms grouped by the package are not as closely related (or functionally cohesive) as they should be. A very high utilization suggests that the subprograms are closely related or functionally cohesive.

In the above scenario we have identified a desirable attribute (cohesion) that we would expect to be present in code that employs packages in constructing ADTs. We have also identified a code property that can assist in measuring the extent to which cohesion is present, e.g. the use of packages in defining ADTs. The measurement approach is based on the extent to which those subprograms (in the ADT) are utilized by importing procedures. That is, to effectively measure the cohesiveness of packages that export subprograms, one must examine the utilization of the subprograms by "withing" units. Intuitively, if the subprograms are sufficiently related, any unit that "withs" the package should use a majority of the subprograms. The indicative metric, calculated on a per package basis, is given by the following formula:

$$\text{Utilization of Packages that Export Subprograms} = \frac{\displaystyle\sum_{\substack{\text{"withs" to package} \\ \text{that export subprograms}}} \text{Subprograms Referenced in Package}}{(\text{Total \# of "withs"}) \cdot \left(\begin{array}{c} \text{\# of Subprograms in} \\ \text{the Package Specification} \end{array}\right)}$$

Hence, the corresponding indicator is

$$\text{COH : DPES} = 5 \cdot \text{Utilization of Package that Exports Subprograms}$$

where the attribute/property pair (denoted COH:DPES) are cohesion and the definition of packages that export subprograms, respectively.

In summary, the OPA Framework provides a formal basis for defining a software quality assessment procedure that includes both code and document products. Using the set of steps described above we have defined 66 code indicators for Ada programs: eight are based on data type information, 12 exploit properties of statement level structures, and 46 reflect characteristic assessments of unit level constructs such as packages, subprograms and so forth. For all 66 indicators, a prototype Ada code analyzer ADALYZER and report generator (RGEN) provide the necessary automation for code analysis, data collection, indicator computation, and reporting of results.

6.2 Attributes of Code Quality

Producing code that is maintainable, reliable and/or reusable is a highly desirable goal. Nonetheless, because such concepts represent abstract amalgamations of many distinct quality characteristics, directly measuring their existence is often difficult, if not impossible. For example, we know that the use of structured data types promotes maintainability through code cohesion (Conway et. al., 1976). On the other hand, if those same data structures are used as parameters in procedure calls, excessive inter-module coupling is likely to be introduced through the passing of extraneous information that is part of the data structure but unused by the called procedure. This use of structured data types has an adverse impact on maintainability (Troy and Zweben 1981).

The paradox illustrated above is a direct reflection of trying to measure quality relative to a concept that is too abstract. Note, however, that the beneficial impact of using structured data types is related to a *cohesive* quality imparted to the code. Similarly, but with a negative effect is the adverse impact of using structured data types that introduces unnecessary inter-module *coupling*. If one views the impact of structured data types relative to these *attributes* of code quality rather than project-level objectives, no paradox exists.

The following subsections enumerate and discuss those code attributes that support product quality assessment from an individual module perspective. The work by Dandekar (1987) and Bundy (1990) serves as the basis for the discussion.

6.2.1 Cohesion

Cohesion is defined to be *the degree to which the tasks performed by a single program module are functionally related.* A cohesive module is a collection of statements and data items that are treated as a whole because they reflect actions and data stores focused on the proper execution of a single function. Through linkages to the software engineering principles of abstraction, information hiding and stepwise refinement, cohesion can be traced as one contributor to the achievement of project-level objectives such as maintainability, reliability and reusability.

Although seven types of cohesion have been identified (Stevens et al., 1974), three are most prominent in reflecting the degree to which a module is cohesive: functional cohesion, sequential cohesion and communicational cohesion. A functionally cohesive module is one in which every processing element is an integral part of, and is essential to, the performance of a single function. Sequential cohesion is characterized by distinct processing elements within a module that combine to form a linear chain of successive or sequential transformations of the data. On the other hand, modules which exhibit communicational cohesion possess code constructs which simply share information in the process of computing an intended function. In terms of module engineering, functional cohesion is the most desirable, followed by sequential and communicational cohesion, respectively.

Understanding the implications of cohesion relative to the achievement of project-level objectives is crucial. Just as crucial, however, is establishing a firm understanding of how the various types of cohesions differ and are reflected in module code – this understanding provides the basis for identifying measurable code properties attesting to the presence or absence of module cohesion.

An Indicator of Cohesion: The Use of Block Statements

Block statements, e.g. `begin/end,` `while` and `for` are control structures that are provided by most imperative languages. By binding code together through the use of blocking statements, code cohesion is enhanced. This conjecture is supported by the observation that statements enclosed in block structures usually define specific functions (or sub-functions) related to the task of the encompassing module.

To measure the extent to which the use of block statements promotes code cohesion, we assume that the ideal module has all of its code enclosed in blocking structures, and then measure that percentage actually placed within such structures. In an attempt to adjust for artificial (or unnatural) cases where: (a) significant amounts of code are enclosed in a single blocking statement, or (b) small amounts of code are enclosed in many block structures, we utilize an additional normalization component based on the expected number of block structures (derived from an average across all modules).

In defining the metric we have elected to measure only code that is enclosed in the outermost (Level 0) blocking structures. Effectively, all nested blocking structures and their respective code are counted as single lines of code within a single blocking structure.

Metric definition:

Let SLOC denote the number of Source Lines of Code (excluding comments) and BS denote Block Structure at Level 0

$$\text{Avg SLOC per BS} = \frac{\text{Total SLOCs in all modules}}{\text{Total number of BSs in all modules}}$$

$$\text{Expected Number of BSs} = \frac{\text{Total SLOCs in Module}}{\text{Avg SLOCs per BS}}$$

$$\text{Metric Formula} = \frac{\text{Total SLOC Enclosed by BS}}{\text{Total SLOC of Module}} \bullet \frac{\text{Expected Number of BSs}}{\text{Number of BSs in Module}}$$

A proposed indicator reflecting *Cohesion relative to the Use of Block Structures*:

COH : UOBS = −5 + 10 •* (Metric Formula)

In the above computation we do constrain the value of the metric formula to be between 0 and 1. Consequently the range of the indicator value is between −5 and 5 with 5 denoting the highest cohesion and −5, the least value for cohesion. A 5 is achieved if the module under consideration has at least the number of expected block structures at level 0 and all of its code is enclosed by those block structures.

Other Properties Influencing Cohesion

Additional properties influencing cohesion include:

- Use of switches as parameters   (−)
- Use of controls structures   (+)
- Multiple entry points in a module   (−)
- Multiple exit points from loops   (−)
- Multiple exit points from modules   (−)
- Number of calling modules   (+)
- Excessive number of called modules   (−)
- Modularization   (+)
- Definition of declaration packages   (+)
- Definition of packages that export subprograms (+)

Properties labeled with a "+" signify that they denote a beneficial (or positive) impact of a property on an attribute. Conversely, a "−" indicates a negative impact.

6.2.2 Complexity

We define complexity *as the degree or complication of a system or system component, determined by such factors as the number and intricacy of interfaces, the number and intricacy of conditional branches, the level of nesting, the types of data structures, and other system characteristics.* In some sense complexity is an abstract measure of work associated with understanding a software component. All participants in software development are subject to mistakes–programmers, analysts and designers. The underlying reason for mistakes is the significant complexity of the proposed problem. Or, from a different perspective, mistakes occur because of the limited capacity of humans to understand complexity.

Factors affecting complexity are: (a) the amount of information that must be understood correctly, (b) the accessibility of information, and (c) the structure of information (Yourdon and Constantine, 1978). The "amount of information" corresponds directly to the number of statements or arguments that are presented to the software engineer at one time. For software, this factor is related to the size of a program module. The "accessibility of information" refers to the availability of information about a software component that enhances the understanding necessary for writing or interpreting the code correctly. For example, code comments and development documentation reduce module complexity. Finally, "structure information" captures the impact that presentation format has on complexity. For example, code presented in a linear fashion, rather than nested, is less complex. Similarly, information is less complex if represented in a positive form rather than in a negative one. Both of these concepts are directly applicable to writing and understanding code.

Because the attribute of complexity is the most difficult to define, for illustrative purposes we include instances of each of the three factors in its definition. This inclusion also underscores the absolute necessity of having a clear understanding of: (a) what constitutes module complexity and (b) what measurable module properties indicate reduced or excessive complexity.

An Indicator of Complexity: Mixing the Order of Parameters within a Call Statement

Within languages like Ada the programmer has the option to pass parameter values according to defined position or by naming the parameter value to correspond to the formal name in the called module. The use of named parameters is beneficial when one elects to employ default values defined by the called module. This capability can be abused, however, if the programmer elects to pass parameters in a sequence that differs from that defined in the formal parameter list of the called module. The reordering of parameters is possible through the use of named parameters. Nonetheless, such decisions contribute to confusion and incomprehensibility, and thereby, add to the complexity of the module and to the overall program.

The proposed measurement approach examines each call statement within a given module and compares the order of each parameter list with the ordering specified by the formal argument list defined by the called module.

If any of the parameter lists differ from the defined formal argument list, then complexity is being increased. This measure is to be tempered relative to the total number of call statements in the module.

Metric Definition:

$$\text{Proportion of Call Statements with Reordered Parameters} = \frac{\text{Total Number of Call Statements with Parameter Lists whose Ordering Differs from the Corresponding Formal Argument List}}{\text{Total Number of Call Statements}}$$

A proposed indicator reflecting *Complexity relative to Mixing the Order of Parameter in Call Statements:*

$$\text{COM: MOPCS} = -5 \cdot \left(\begin{array}{c} \text{Proportion of Call Statements} \\ \text{with Reordered Parameters} \end{array} \right)$$

Note that the range of the proposed indicator, COM : MOPCS, is between −5 and 0. This range reflects the fact that the presence of a call statement with reordered parameters can only add to the complexity of a module. Effectively, the absence of such call statements, i.e. an indicator value of 0, contributes neither to enhancing nor diminishing module complexity.

Other Properties Influencing Complexity

Given the attention directed toward program complexity, the various forms suggested and the numerous metrics advocated, the recognition of many properties that can be tied to this attribute is not surprising. No doubt, others beyond those identified in this work could be selected.

Additional properties influencing complexity include:

- Use of control structures   (+)
- Excessive nesting of control structures   (−)
- Use of dynamic structures   (−)
- Use of meaningful names for modules and variables   (+)
- Use of GOTOs   (−)
- Use of negative compound booleans   (−)
- Use of block comments   (+)
- Program length   (−)

- Use of embedded alternate language   (−)
- Use of code indentation   (+)
- Use of recursive code   (−)
- Multiple entry and exit points for module   (−)
- Use of both default parameters and positional notation (−)
- Use of parameter notation   (+)
- Mixing the order of parameter lists   (−)
- Use of both positional and name notation in a single module call (−)
- Use of record discriminants   (+)
- Use of exception handlers   (+)

6.2.3 Coupling

Coupling is defined as *the measure of the interdependence among modules in a computer program.* Coupling results when an element of code references a location in memory which is not defined in the encompassing module. In more general terms, coupling occurs when elements of code in two distinct modules reference the same location in memory. Two common situations that give rise to coupling are: (a) the use of global variables and (b) the use of parameters to share information.

As a rule one strives to reduce coupling. The interdependence among modules can adversely affect the modifiability of a module through what is known as the "ripple effect period". The ripple effect occurs when one makes a change in Module A and inadvertently introduces changes in other modules. For example suppose that Modules A and B share data through a globally defined *integer* variable C. Suppose further that the type of C is changed to *real* to accommodate algorithmic changes in Module A. The impact of that change will "ripple" down to all other modules that reference C, e.g. Module B. The minimization of coupling is a direct result of applying the principle of information hiding, for example. Applying other principles can affect coupling as well.

The degree of coupling among modules is primarily related to three factors: the type of dependent connection, the size of the connection and the type of communication permitted through the communication. Connection types can be partitioned into two categories: (1) connections that address or refer to a module as an entity by its name, i.e. passing information through a *procedure call*, and (2) connections that refer to internal elements of a module, e.g. the use of non-local (or global) variables for sharing information. Connections of Type 1 are more effective in reducing coupling. Connection size refers to the amount of information that is passed (shared) between two modules – the more extensive the sharing, the higher the coupling. Finally, the third factor recognizes the difference between information in the form of data versus control. Data coupling is coupling introduced by sharing simple information such as computational items. Control coupling stems from the sharing of information through which decisions are made in a subordinate (or superordinate) module. Typically, such control information is termed as a "flag" or "switch". Coupling associated with the passing of data information is less severe than that caused by the passing of control information.

An Indicator of Coupling: The Use of Structured Data Types as Parameters

As stated earlier the use of structured data types can have a beneficial or detrimental impact depending on the form of use. In particular, when data structures are passed as parameters, seldom is every data element needed by the receiving module. In effect, those extraneous data elements introduce unnecessary inter-module coupling.

To capture the impact that the use of structured data parameters has on inter-module coupling, one examines each parameter list to determine what percentage of parameters are, in fact, structured data elements. That is, for all calls within any given module the proposed measure relates the actual number of structured data type parameters to the total number (structured and primitive data elements).

Metric Definition:

$$\text{Proportion of Structured Data Types Used as Parameters} = \frac{\text{Number of Structured Data Types Parameters}}{\text{Total Number of Parameters}}$$

A proposed indicator reflecting *Coupling relative to the use of Structured Data Types used as Parameters:*

$$\text{COUP} : \text{STDP} = -5 \bullet \text{Proportion of Structured Data Types Used as Parameters}$$

Note that the values for the indicator COUP : STDP range between –5 to 0, indicating that the use of structured data types as parameters can have only a detrimental impact on coupling as an attribute affecting software quality.

Other Properties Influencing Coupling

Excessive inter-module coupling is often cited as reflecting poor design. Clearly, a code indicator of poor design provides information a posteriori. Before taking the action of reviewing the design, one would want to have additional evidence that such a costly decision is warranted. Additional indicators of coupling include:

- Use of global variables   (–)
- Use of switches as parameters   (–)
- Use of parameterless procedure calls   (–)
- Multiple entry points to a module   (–)
- Number of calling modules   (–)
- Types of parameters
  - Control   (–)
  - Data   (+)
- Relying on upper level modules to handle raised exceptions   (–)

6.2.4 Ease of Change

We define ease of change as *the ease with which software accommodates enhancements or extensions*. Ease of change is often referred to by other authors as: (a) expandability – the ability to provide for the expansion of data or program function), or (b) changeability – the ease with which the logic of a program can be changed.

In general, code is never a static object – over time, changes, extensions, enhancements and expansions are required. Changes, and in particular the ease of change, must be viewed from two related perspectives: (1) when the code is first produced and (2) when the code is being modified.

When a system is first being developed, one should design with change in mind. Where appropriate, for example, data dictionaries and data base management systems should be exploited. Data dictionaries provide common naming conventions and data descriptions which are then combined to form the record structures used by all code modules. Modular design helps isolate and encapsulate individual functions, thereby minimizing the scope and impact of changing any one particular function. During the coding phase, the use of sound software engineering principles such as information hiding, structured programming and stepwise refinement are critical to supporting ease of change.

When a code unit is being modified, the changes should not adversely impact the ease of future change. This latter point is particularly crucial for those systems that are expected to have a long lifetime and to evolve over an extended period of time. More specifically, maintenance personnel must focus on changes that are controlled and carefully monitored, while adhering to those same principles used in the initial product development.

An Indicator of Ease of Change: The Use of Symbolic Constants

If a constant is used several times in a module, it is preferable to define that value as a symbolic constant and then refer to its associated identifier wherever the constant value is needed. Such an approach has two major advantages over using constant values in every appearance: (1) it permits one to associate a meaningful name with a value, e.g. EOF for cntrl-D, and (2) if the value needs to be changed at a later point in time, a single change of value is sufficient.

To measure the impact of the use of symbolic constants relative to ease of change, two pieces of information must be considered: (1) the number of symbolic constants currently being used in the module, and (2) the potential use of additional symbolic constants. The latter can be determined by counting the number of non-symbolic constants that are used multiple times within the given module. Relative to ease of change, the ideal module always uses symbolic constants in lieu of multiple references to non-symbolic constants.

Metric Definition:

$$\text{Proportional use of Symbolic Constants} = \frac{\text{Number of Symbolic Constants Defined}}{\text{Number of Distinct Uses of Multiple References to Non-Symbolic Constants} + \text{Number of Symbolic Constants Defined}}$$

A proposed indicator reflecting *Ease Of Change relative to the Use of Symbolic Constants:*

$$\text{EOC : USC} = 5 \bullet \text{Proportional use of Symbolic Constants}$$

The range of values for the indicator, EOC : USC, is (0, 5). With this particular indicator the use of symbolic constants in a module can only have a beneficial impact on ease of change, hence, the consequent values are zero (0) or greater.

Other Properties Influencing Ease of Change

Additional properties influencing of ease of change include:

- Use of dynamic structures   (+)
- Use of modularization   (+)
- Use of global variables   (−)
- Number of modules called   (−)
- Definition of declaration units   (+)
- Insufficient decomposition of declaration units   (−)
- Definition of units that export subprograms   (+)

6.2.5 Readability

Readability can be defined as *the difficulty in understanding the function(s) of a software component and how that functionality is realized by that software component.* We strive for code that is readable, i.e., understandable. The more readable a code module, the easier it is to understand what function(s) the code unit performs and how that function(s) is realized in the code itself.

Many factors affect code readability. Most prominent among such factors are those related to comments and code structure. Code comments, for example, can be placed at the beginning of a module to provide a natural language description of its functionality. Comments can also be interspersed throughout the code to provide insights into how the functionality is being realized. Obviously, in the absence of comments, maintenance personnel must rely on somewhat cryptic code to determine functionality and module structure. Even more detrimental, however, is the presence of incorrect comments. Incorrect (or inaccurate) comments are often an artifact of modifying code without appropriately changing the corresponding comments. Such comments are likely to mislead maintenance personnel and cause the code to be misinterpreted.

Code structure includes several items that promote readability. For example, code indentation is useful to represent nested conditionals and loops, that is, conditionals or loops that are "subordinate" to other conditionals or loops. The use of structured programming constructs, the avoidance of negative compound conditionals, and the separation of an IF statement's true-part and else-part all represent aspects of a structured approach to coding which promotes readability.

An Indicator of Readability: Use of GOTOs

As stated above code structure plays an important role in the readability of software modules. That structure can assume either physical characteristics, like code indentation, or logical ones, e.g. the use of GOTOs. GOTOs first appeared in FORTRAN in the late 1950s and have been incorporated (although reluctantly so) in many languages since. GOTOs are an unconditional runtime branch to another location in the program. This language "feature" represents the antithesis of structured programming concepts. GOTOs destroy code readability by introducing unstructured control within a module. Inordinate use of GOTOs results in what is known as "spaghetti code."

Because the detrimental impact of GOTOs is absolute, measuring its effect is relatively easily. We propose a simple metric that decreases a module's readability factor in direct proportion to the number of GOTOs found.

Metric Definition:

Extent of GOTO Usage = 2 • Number of GOTOs

A proposed indicator reflecting *Readability relative to the use of GOTOs:*

READ : GOTO = max (−5, 0 − Extent of GOTO usage)

Because of the absolute value associated with this proposed indicator, its value is constrained to the range (−5, 0). While this penalty might seem harsh, consensus in the software engineering community supports such a view.

Other Properties Influencing Readability

Additional properties influencing readability include:

- Use of control structures   (+)
- Use of symbolic constants   (+)
- Multiple statements on one line   (−)
- Use of meaningful names for routines and variables   (+)
- Multiple exit points from loops   (−)
- Modules exceeding one printed page in length   (−)
- Use of block comments   (+)

- Excessive use of single line comments   (−)
- Use of parenthesized expressions   (+)
- Overloading of operator or subprogram names   (−)
- Definition of modules that execute concurrently   (−)
- Mixing order of parameter lists   (−)
- Use of parameters with name notation   (+)

6.2.6 Traceability

Traceability is defined as *the software (code and documentation) attribute that provides a link from requirements to the implemented program* (Arthur 1985). In other words it is the ease in retracing the complete history of a software component from its current state to its design inception.

As a system evolves conventional wisdom mandates the verification of requirements to design and design to code. Traceability characteristics, captured in development documents and artifacts such as the software development folder, are indispensable in the verification process. Similarly, the capability to trace code elements to their originating requirements supports an evaluation process that ensures the necessity for inclusion of all such elements.

In addition to supporting the development process, traceability is a critical component in the execution of software maintenance. In particular, proposed code and design changes must be thoroughly researched to determine their impact on other systems elements and the overall set of currently defined requirements.

Clearly, design documents that include traceability matrices and references to other documents assist in providing traceability. References to called procedures and code comments provide additional traceability artifacts.

An Indicator of Traceability: Use of Comments Referencing Project Documents and "Who Called Me"

Measuring traceability based on code attributes relies primarily on comments that reference: (a) project documentation, and (b) other calling modules. Unlike previously defined indicators, assessing traceability through comment references relies more on content analysis rather than data item counts. Consequently, the data collection is, by necessity, a time consuming, manual process. Nonetheless, well placed code comments provide the necessary links relating sections of code to corresponding design and requirement specifications. Moreover, comments that describe calling sequences, and in particular, those which describe "who calls me" provide traceability to higher-level modules, and hence, to higher-level functions supported by the module being examined.

Similar to the immediately preceding indicator, measuring traceability through the use of use of appropriate comment references relies primarily on a simple count, that is, the number of references to project documentation and to calling modules.

Metric Definition:

$$
\begin{array}{ccccc}
\text{Number of} & & \text{Number of} & & \text{Number of} \\
\text{Comment} & = & \text{References to} & + & \text{References to} \\
\text{References} & & \text{Project} & & \text{Calling Modules} \\
& & \text{Documentation} & &
\end{array}
$$

A proposed indicator reflecting *Traceability relative to the use of Comment References*:

TRAC : NOCR = min (Number of Comment References, 5)

Other Properties Influencing Traceability

Traceability is an easily understood attribute. Consequently, little confirmation through other properties is either needed or possible. Additional properties that impact traceability include:

- Consistency in the use of variable names in code and documentation (+)
- Organizational consistency between code and documentation.   (+)

6.2.7 Well-defined Interfaces

An interface is defined as a shared boundary where autonomous systems interact (communicate) with each other (Dale and Orshalick, 1983). While interfaces exist in many different forms, e.g. hardware/hardware, hardware/software and software/humanware, relative to software quality assessment we focus our attention primarily on those interfaces that support communication among software components. Subsequently, a well-defined interface can be defined as *the definitional clarity and completeness of a shared boundary between a pair of software components*.

Guidelines for a well-defined interface suggest that a module's interface should be defined and used so that:

1. all communication passes through the interface,

2. parameters lists are kept small, and

3. inputs are separated from the outputs (Marca, 1984).

The first guideline requires that: (a) each input and output be definitively identified and described in detail, (b) all requisite data be passed when a module is invoked, and (c) all results are passed back to the calling module when the called module completes execution. The most common violation of the first guideline is the use of global variables for the sharing of information among modules. The second guideline underscores the necessity of keeping parameter lists small. Stevens, for example, suggests that the number of parameters should not exceed three or four – effectively, minimizing the number of parameters tends to improve the clarity and simplicity of the interface (Stevens, 1981). Finally, the third guideline stipulates (or implies) that "in", "out" and "in/out" parameters be easily distinguishable. Languages such as Pascal and Ada support and enforce such classification.

An Indicator of Well-defined Interfaces: The Use of Parameterless Procedures

The interface between two modules is defined by the data elements passed between them. An explicit indication and description of those data elements is crucial to the creation of a well-defined interface. Nonetheless, modules are often invoked using parameterless procedure calls. Implicit in such invocations is that communications are occurring through the use of global or non-local variables. Consequently, the information exchanged between the calling and the called module is difficult to determine; hence, the interface characteristics between the two modules are obscured.

To measure the impact of parameterless calls on well-defined interfaces we require two data elements: (1) the number of parameterless calls, and (2) the number of calls that have parameters. Relative to well-defined interfaces the latter count is used to temper the negative effect of the former.

Metric Definition:

$$\text{Proportion of Parameterless Calls} = \frac{\text{Number of Parameterless Calls}}{\text{Number of Calls with Parameters} + \text{Number of Parameterless Calls}}$$

A proposed indicator reflecting a *Well Defined Interface relative to the Use of Parameterless Calls*:

WDI: UOPC = − 5 • Proportion of Parameterless Calls

Other Properties Influencing Well-defined Interfaces

Additional properties that influence well-defined interfaces include:

- Use of global variables   (−)
- Use of structured data types as parameters   (−)
- Use of excessive number of parameters   (−)
- Definition of default parameters   (+)
- Definition of units that export subprograms   (+)

6.2.8 Attributes of Code Quality: A Summary

In summary, seven attributes of code quality are described above. The intent of this discussion is to

- present a sample of those characteristics that contribute to code quality,
- discuss code quality relative to measures that employ observable, concrete data elements, and
- promote the thesis that "observable properties of the code exist that attest to the *presence* or *absence* of attributes such as cohesion, coupling, ease of change, readability, complexity, traceability and well-defined interfaces."

Those observable properties, coupled with individual attributes, form the basis for defining code indicators. The OPA Framework links computed indicator values to the use of appropriate principles in the development process, and finally, the employment of principles to the achievement of project-level objectives. Interpreted within the OPA Framework, these indicators support decision processes at the software engineering, software management and project management levels.

6.3 Automated Collection of Code Indicators

Experience has shown that manually collecting data to compute code indicator values is labor- intensive and error prone. The OPA approach utilizes many contrasting and confirming SQIs. Partly because of the number but also because of our original intent, the data items required to compute the SQIs are simple and easily obtained. Consequently, automated data collection is facilitated, as is the metric computation associated with each SQI for code. A prototype Ada code analyzer (ADALYZER) analyzes code based on its compilation order and extracts the necessary data items to compute 66 code indicators.

6.4 Interpretation, Decision and Actions

As stated in Section 2.3 the OPA Framework stresses assessment through the employment of multiple confirming and contrasting indicators of quality. Each indicator focuses on the measurement of one particular characteristic of quality. Taken together, the full set of indicator measures provide an accumulation of evidence attesting to the extent to which product quality has been achieved. The multiple indicator approach follows the rationale that no single measure of quality exists. Moreover, it recognizes the fact no two modules are expected to exhibit the same quality characteristics.

In general, code assessment provides an "after the fact" judgment of quality. Nonetheless, it can provide crucial insights supporting the development of better quality products in the future. If the development process is based on an incremental approach, those insights can have an immediate beneficial impact.

From a code perspective, software quality assessment is focused at the unit level. That is, each module is individually examined for quality attributes. If a particular attribute for that module receives a low rating, the software engineer examines the indicators contributing to the aggregated attribute value, isolating the indicator (or indicators) that contributes to the low score. Because each indicator is defined to include the rationale behind its measurement, the software engineer is guided through a reasoned explanation as to why the module is judged to be inadequate. Based on that explanation, a preliminary set of actions can be formulated to correct the inadequacies. Since the definition of each indicator includes all code properties contributing to its assessment, the preliminary set of corrective actions can be focused and refined to address the precise characteristic(s) contributing to the module's low quality rating.

In addition to providing the software engineer with the crucial insight necessary to identify and correct software quality problems, the definitional structure of each indicator promotes additional education. Through periodic examination of the indicator characteristics, the software engineer is continually exposed to those basic elements and activities that contribute to the development of a quality product.

An Examination of Indicator Values and Their Aggregation

7

The OPA Framework relies on indicators, defined and developed in the tradition of social science research. Indicators are surrogates that are directly measurable; whereas the attributes are concepts that do not admit to direct measurement. The value and benefits derived from a software measurement program accrue in time as experience enables the user to gain confidence in the values and to recognize the signals embodied in them.

A well designed quality measurement program relies on instrumentation throughout the development or maintenance process. Confirming and contrasting indicators can present a more holistic picture than selected metrics in isolation. Presentations using aggregated values and trend accumulations in graphs or tables can be especially effective.

7.1 Using and Interpreting Indicator Values

Recall that an indicator measurement reflects an attribute and property relationship that is described as an attribute/property pair in Section 2. More specifically, the indicator value portrays the degree to which the property provides evidence that the attribute is present in the product or process. Some attributes can give evidence only of the absence of an attribute (computation of their value is limited to the range 0 to −5). Others can support only the presence of an attribute, ranging from 0 to +5. Still others give evidence of both the absence and the presence and can take on the full range of values $(-5, +5)$.

The employment of software quality indicators within the OPA Framework results in measures that are singularly focused; that is, each captures one aspect of software quality. Similarly, each aggregated measure is associated with a single attribute, principle or objective. Relative to the interpretation of these measures, we offer a few helpful hints of guidance.

1. An indicator value in the interval around "0" (roughly -0.5 to $+0.5$) implies that either: (a) no significant basis for judging quality is found, or (b) equal evidence supporting both beneficial and detrimental judgments of quality is found. These two cases can be distinguished by examining the variability among values contributing to the aggregate measure. High variability in itself is a warning that should be heeded.

2. Each indicator has a recognized "critical component" that if absent renders the indicator non-computable. For example, a property that is used in the denominator of an automated metric computation and whose absence results in a zero (0) value is deemed a critical component. In this situation, continuing with the metric computation results in a "divide by zero error." Subsequently, during the computation of each indicator, if a critical component is absent, that indicator is assigned a default value of "0", i.e., no basis for judgment exists. During the interpretation process one must be aware that an abundance of "default zeros" included in aggregate values can obscure quality assessment by lowering potentially high measures of quality and by raising potentially low measures.

3. The OPA Framework requires the users of the procedure to define what quality means by the prioritization of objectives on any given project. Objectives can be competitive and mutually inhibitive as well as mutually supportive. A failure to assign priorities to objectives represents an abdication of responsibility for product and process quality. Further, the interpretation of quality is subject to serious misgiving in the absence of a clear statement of what represents quality for a given project.

4. The OPA Framework enables only relative measures of quality; anyone claiming to have a procedure for an absolute measurement is immediately suspect. Sufficient differences exist among software projects that drawing comparisons across projects from entirely different organizations should be done only with great caution and clear understanding that homogeneity in the statistical sense is not likely to allow such a comparison. Only with a database compiled of several (or many) projects can a single organization hope to deal with valid statistical comparisons across projects.

5. Because no database of experience yet exists, interpreting quality measures in an absolute sense must be avoided. For example, the absolute difference in the quality of a module or system that receives a score of 1.7 versus one that receives a 2.4 is unknown. What is known, however, is that the latter module or system is considered to have evidence supporting the claim that its quality exceeds that of the former.

7.2 Integrating Code, Documentation and Process Quality Indicators in a Software Quality Measurement Program

The initiation of any project is a period of excitement and high expectations. For those administering a software quality management program based on the OPA Framework, specific tasks must be accomplished.

- Key project personnel must be briefed (possibly educated) on the premises of the Framework and the procedures to be used.

- Decisions on measurement points, procedures and responsibilities must be made.

- Reporting frequency and format should be agreed upon so that the measurement group maintains the needed independence and feedback is provided for process improvement.

The roles of the three types of indicators (code, documentation and process) are illustrated in a variation of *Fig. 2.3*, which is given in *Fig. 7.1*. Keep in mind

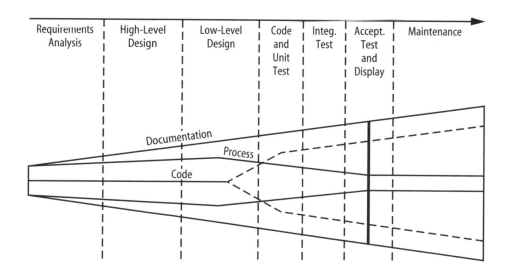

Figure 7.1 *The importance of indicator sources to software quality prediction and assessment in the OPA framework*

that *Fig. 7.1* is an illustration of a "typical" software project and represents no specific development or maintenance effort. Nevertheless, we find it instructive in portraying the supportive roles of the sources examined as they change with time and project phasing.

Initially, the reliance on documentation as a source of data is by necessity; nothing else exists beyond a *Software Engineering Manual* (*SEM*) or a *Software Development Plan* (*SDP*). The former provides information on how well the organization understands the needs for producing quality software; the latter should layout the specific process to be followed for the given project. *Figure 7.1* shows the accumulative sources of indicator information among the three to take distinctly different shapes.

- Documentation data represent the only sources initially and the data increase from the early level (*SEM* and *SDP*) throughout the development phases with the increase occurring at a smaller rate during the in-service support period.

- Process data, derived primarily from the SEM and SDP, increase also but at a lesser rate than document data. (Recall that document quality is judged on format, presentation and content; while process quality focuses more narrowly on content.)

- Toward the end of the detailed design phase, code begins to emerge and rapidly becomes a major source, continuing throughout the coding and testing phases but never at the rate seen during code and unit test.

The consequences to be drawn from *Fig. 7.1* are that the Process Indicators, with some support from Document Quality Indicators, provide the basis for prediction during the development project when changes can be made without exorbitant cost. The quality assessment relies heavily on the products of the code creation, unit test and integration testing phases. In a few cases, indicators may serve their usefulness and be discarded. In other cases, an indicator value may be updated as newer data becomes available. Also, we have the indicator that continues to be used but whose importance may diminish simply because of new data emerging, giving rise to new indicators.

An organization might choose to follow a pattern of weighting indicators based on the perceptions of their importance in either prediction or assessment. A measurement program that provides an automated follow-up scheme, assigning weights based on past predictive capability, is not difficult to envision. Clearly, the integration and interpretation of indicator values are likely to differ exceedingly among organizations, but, hopefully, within an organization, a consistent, accepted procedure is followed.

Prediction and Assessment: Differences in Goals

This book is intended to provide guidance in the creation of a software quality measurement program utilizing the OPA Framework and Software Quality Indicators. Two points of emphasis throughout the description are: (1) the evolutionary nature of large, complex software systems, and (2) the project perspective supported by software measurement. Both are important in their influences on the presentation. Large software systems, be they "mission-critical," also termed "embedded systems," "real-time systems," "time-critical systems" or "automated information systems" (AIS), exhibit complexities that can overwhelm the typical software engineer, systems engineer or project manager. Measurement, or the more popular term "software metrics," offers a means of dealing with those problems that arise in the creation of any large, complex system. The project perspective can apply equally to mission-critical or AIS systems, although within DoD, the term is associated more with the former. Indicative of the project perspective is the focus on objectives, and for software-intensive projects, the prioritization among software engineering objectives.

Coupling the evolutionary nature of large, complex systems with the project perspective introduces another perception: the diminution of the distinction between development and sustainment (maintenance). An evolutionary system passes through alternating periods of emphasis on creation (adding of functionality) and consolidation (correcting and perfecting the functional form) several times during its lifetime. Unless imposed by contractual arrangements, the distinction of the initial development activities from the subsequent sustaining and supporting activities is of little importance. Differences in the application of the OPA Framework or implications in its use can stem in part from three sources: (1) the process model(s) used over the life of the system, (2) the limitation to assessment without prediction, and (3) contractual constraints for separating development and sustainment.

8.1 Effects of Process Models

While the OPA Framework originated with no underlying process model influence, use of the procedure must be patterned to the model governing the development process. This patterning or tailoring does not detract from the benefits of measurement, but does alter to some degree the cost and scheduling of measurement activities.

8.1.1 The Waterfall Model

The version of the Waterfall Model shown in *Fig. 8.1*, taken from Lavender (1988) is that on which DOD-STD-2167 was based and serves well for our discussion of software quality measurement in such a process. Note that only the development process is shown in the model. Within a development process described by the classical Waterfall Model, the prioritization of objectives should precede the requirements definition. Process measurement could initiate even earlier through examination of a SEI Capability Maturity Model evaluation, a *Software Engineering Manual* (a *Software Standards and Procedures Manual*), or a *Software Development Plan*. If a *Software Configuration Management Plan* and *Software Quality Evaluation Plan* are generated, then both should be examined also. Process measurement following generation of the *Software Requirements Specification* (*SRS*) and the *Interface Requirements Specification* (*IRS*) focuses on attributes induced from two principles: Abstraction and Concurrent Documentation. Process and document assessment is conducted concurrently, and the documentation products begin to assume a more predominant role. The complementary relationship over time between process and document assessment is illustrated earlier in *Fig. 2.3* and also in *Fig. 7.1*.

We advocate the application of process assessment prior to the review points shown in *Fig. 8.1* for each of the software components undergoing review. Discussion of process difficulties should be an agenda item for each review. Comparison of the reviews for each software component, conducted by the SQA representative for the project, can point to common process difficulties and potential improvements.

Clearly, the expected predictive capability should improve as the project matures. The combined process and product data increases, providing a more accurate reflection of the quality. Nevertheless, changes in requirements for example can cause major redesign that could affect the quality of a specific software component and infuse uncertainty into the predictions.

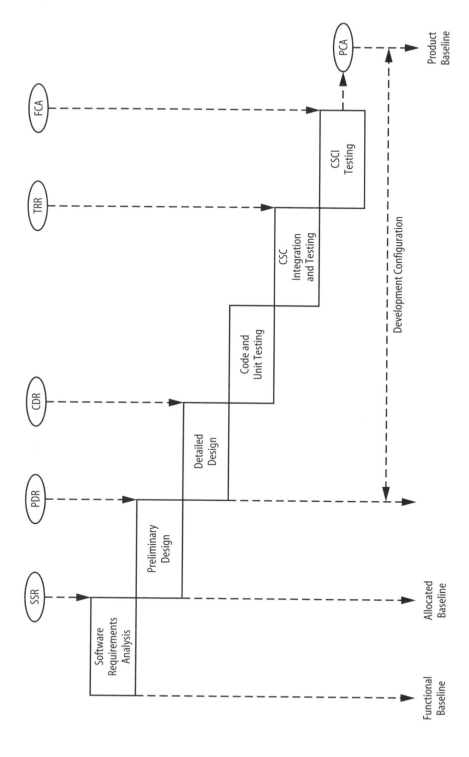

Figure 8.1 The software development life cycle for DoD-STD-2167 (from Lavender, 1988, p. 181)

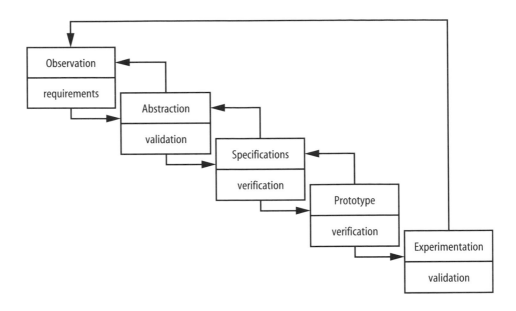

Figure 8.2 *Gidding's domain dependent software life-cycle model (from Giddings, 1984, p.431)*

8.1.2 The Domain-dependent Life-cycle Model

Pictured in *Fig. 8.2*, this model offered by Giddings (1984) is similar to the Waterfall Model in its portrayal of a sequential succession of stages. However, the culmination of the activities with a prototype that is the subject of experimentation leads to feedback for restatement of requirements and repetition of the cycle. The Domain-Dependent Model corresponds more faithfully to the characterization of "evolutionary" software; no clear distinction is made between development and sustainment.

The OPA Framework would be applied from the initial specification of requirements throughout each succeeding phase. As with the Waterfall Model, an organization gains experience with the Framework and, through comparison with prior projects, recognizes potential early problems in time to take corrective actions. A major responsibility of the OPA Framework is to gauge any major shifts in quality as the project progresses. An experienced organization would set quantitative values that would govern test and release decisions. Note that little is explicitly stated about testing – unit versus integration or the point of system acceptance testing. A software quality measurement program could play a major role in both test and configuration management decisions.

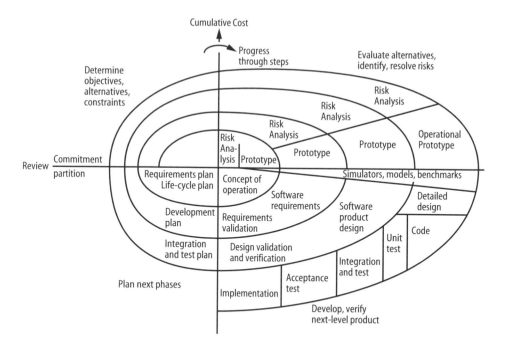

Figure 8.3 *The spiral model (Bohem, 1986)*

8.1.3 Boehm's Spiral Model

The Spiral Model (Boehm, 1986), shown in *Fig. 8.3*, portrays the cyclic nature of a process that assures requirements validation before production of the delivered system. If the *rapid prototyping* technique is strictly applied, then no quality measurement should be applied until the delivered system detailed design is initiated. (With rapid prototyping the definition of each prototype –design and code – is discarded, and only the knowledge gained is conserved to apply to the design of the next prototype.) Application of the OPA Framework following the operational prototype would take a course similar to that used in the Waterfall Model.

If the *evolutionary prototyping* approach were invoked, then quality measurement would begin at some point in the prototype development but not necessarily with the first. More likely, that prototype judged to provide required functionality in the form to be used in the delivered system would be the point where measurement activities would initiate. (Some would argue that this is the operational prototype in both cases, but others would argue to the contrary.)

8.2 Software Reuse

Reusability is an objective in the OPA Framework. Software reuse – a major benefit of the object-oriented programming paradigm – is touted as realizing significant savings in cost and time. Reused code is also viewed as having higher reliability. What guidelines should be followed in applying the OPA Framework to existing software, often described as "Commercial-Off-The-Shelf" (COTS) or "Not Developed Internally" (NDI)?

At first glance, the measurement task appears to be one of assessment only: analyze the code. No prediction is possible nor is it warranted. We can know very little about the process activities leading to the candidate components for reuse. Such a view is fraught with danger.

Two points should be understood with regard to the measurement of quality of COTS or NDI software: (1) unless both function and technology are essentially unchanged, the proportion of cases where code can be directly adapted and used without change is *very low*, and (2) the key to the degree of adaptation required for reuse is the match between the intended purpose of the reused software and its *original purpose*. Thus, the importance of measuring the supporting documentation – the requirements document, design specifications, user manuals, etc. – cannot be over-emphasized. Certainly, the code can be analyzed, and the automatic analysis of code alone seems a viable and inexpensive strategy. However, subjecting only the code to measurement provides a potentially deceptive result: an initial component with very high quality may have to undergo such transformation, perhaps unassisted by the supporting documentation, that the final result bears little resemblance in its quality profile to the original.

Development documentation and test results may be difficult to obtain for COTS and NDI software, but every effort should be made to do so. At the least, an effort should be made to obtain surrogate information; i.e. deployment defect data, customer reactions, user reviews, etc. While the measurement of document quality is likely to be manual, slow and costly, the confidence in the conclusions regarding software quality should be considerably enhanced.

8.3 Sustaining Responsibilities and Quality Measurement

Common with many DOD systems is the contractual separation of the development and sustainment activities. Also known as "maintenance" or "post-deployment support," sustainment includes those activities that have been categorized as software maintenance in four forms by Swanson (1976):

- corrective: the correction of faults in a software system,
- perfective: the improvement in functionality of a software system to meet current requirements better,
- preventive: the addition of facilities to make a software system more robust, and
- adaptive: the addition of functionality to a software system to accommodate changing requirements.

Some authors prefer to lump perfective and preventive together to list only three forms.

Hopefully, the sustaining organization has been involved closely during the development activities. In the best of worlds, the OPA Framework has been employed during development, and the transition of measurement responsibilities to the sustaining organization is simply a part of the larger transfer. The remainder of this section describes the practical problems and possible alleviating actions if that is not the case, or, worse yet, no measurement program has been in effect.

8.3.1 Initial Assessment

Two important questions for the sustaining organization are: (1) What is the expected life of the delivered software system? and (2) How extensive is the document set delivered as part of the software system? In general, the longer the system life, the greater the need for added functionality (adaptive maintenance) and the more extensive the document set required to support changing requirements effectively, expeditiously, and with acceptable costs. For a long-lived software system, the quality of the delivered product is determined by the quality of the documentation more than the quality of the code. Many have learned, and continue to learn, this lesson the hard way.

Applying the OPA Framework to the delivered product – the document set and the code – provides an initial characterization of the system. While little can be said in absolute terms, unless one has experience in applying the OPA Framework to past systems, the relative values of the document and code indicators help to identify potential trouble points – those components that represent the "soft" spots. These data can assist in personnel assignments: put the best people on the worst components. If the evaluation reveals that the documentation is not current (a very typical occurrence), then the decision to reverse engineer the detailed design specification could be a viable option. The intent in the initial assessment is to enable the sustainment organization to decide if the delivered system is "a pig in a poke" and, if so, begin to separate the bacon from the wrapping.

8.3.2 Continuing Assessment

A quality measurement program can be more beneficial in the sustainment phase than in development. Some may be surprised by such an assertion, but the truth lies in the ability to combat the natural tendency of a software system to lose quality. Deteriorating quality stems from the potential loss of design integrity (clean partitioning of functionality), design congruity (interfaces permitting well-defined communications) and the introduction of errors as changes are made. By measuring the proposed changes, the sustaining organization can hopefully maintain or even improve the quality assessment. Functional changes (adaptive maintenance) can be evaluated in terms of their effect on system quality. The price paid for added functionality in terms of reduced quality is a strong argument that is seldom available for current systems.

8.4 The Quality Database and Validity of Indicators

Assessment in measurement refers to the establishment of "what is." Assessment is applied to the existing entity, and quality assessment is motivated by the desire to say "how good is this widget." Prediction, on the other hand, is applied to that which is in the making. By examining certain characteristics, can we predict the quality of the finished product? While both purposes are important in the measurement of quality, assessment is the easier, but still is extremely difficult.

We note that a number of authors (Arthur, 1993; Ashley, 1995; Dunn, 1990) prefer not to define quality but seek to describe it in ways that promote its measurement. We view the perception of quality much like the perception of beauty: quality lies in the eyes of the beholder or, recognizing the scale of commerce in software, the expectations of the customer. We contend that quality cannot be measured in absolute terms, but being able to assess (or predict) the quality of Product X as superior to that of Product Y is the key issue in an acquisition decision. Thus, we rely on relative measures of quality and each organization must establish the procedures to capture and preserve quality measures so as to build a database that represents a major organizational asset. More about software quality follows in Chapter 9.

A quality measurement database evolves through successive projects and products, permitting the comparison and contrast with prior efforts and the prediction of future achievements based on past data. But, does that mean that software quality indicators, once adopted, should be used for all future projects? The all too obvious answer is "No." The use of an SQI should be a specific decision at the inception of each project. At the conclusion of each project each SQI should be reviewed as to its utility in the project and if the utility is judged marginal, an explanation of the contributing factors should be given. This is a responsibility for the Software Quality Assurance (SQA) group within the organization.

Periodically, the SQA group, as part of its auditing function, should review the SQIs used on projects in the past to evaluate their validity. This evaluation should occur more frequently if the organization mandates either a uniform set or a core set of indicators. This validation could take several forms, ranging from face validity – subjective judgment by an expert team – to a statistical approach that is quantitative. The depth of the validation and the consequent cost is dependent on the cost of the measurement program, the contractual requirements between customers and the organization, and the commitment of the organization to software quality. For a thorough and comprehensive description of validation and verification techniques in simulation, which has struggled with this issue much longer than software engineering, see (Balci, 1994).

Software Quality: Views And Purviews

Few topics engender more diversity of view and opinion than "quality." The term is often used with the modifier "high" implied; only an explicit reference to low quality requires a modifier. An assertion such as "that's a quality automobile" or "quality goes in before the name goes on" needs no clarification that *high quality* is intended. What is embodied in the term "quality" or how an assessment intends to measure it are issues that evoke major disagreements. Consider the differences in perceptions and reactions to the assertion, "that person is a quality teacher." The attributes of a teacher that elicit praise by students vary greatly among the evaluators, simply because a match in learning approach and teaching style is the key to a successful experience.

9.1 *Software Quality:* Holy Grail or Eternal Enigma?

Quality as a concept has always provoked questions and debate: Can it be defined? Do differences in understanding admit resolution? Is quality inherently qualitative or does the concept permit quantification?

The accepted, or conventional, meaning of "quality" has undergone transitions. Yet, a view strongly advocated during some period seems not to fade into obscurity; rather, proponents of the most popular position become zealots for a passing fad. A formerly acceptable premise in the form of, "I cannot tell you what it (quality) is, but I can tell you when something has it," is refuted by the assertion that "what you cannot measure you certainly do not understand and cannot hope to manage."

An initial objective of this chapter is to focus on *quality* as a well accepted goal in all endeavors throughout society, but one that is not well understood when the transition from perception to implementation is required. Questions arise quickly, such as: How can quality be described? What can be done to measure quality or changes in quality? Who should be entrusted with the responsibility for quality improvement? Answers to such questions are further complicated when the object of quality concerns shifts from the product of a physical process to that of a mental process. A second objective is to trace the evolution of *software quality* as a goal from its physical roots in manufacturing to the current state. A final objective is to link this evolution with the rationale that girds the OPA framework for software quality measurement.

9.2 What Is "Quality"?

While the question seems natural and simple, answers are diverse, lengthy and often divisive. Further, answers do not seem to be lasting, perhaps reflecting the transition in understanding that accompanies the entity being judged for quality and the context in which the judgment is made.

9.2.1 Philosophy or Economics Provide Answers

Garvin (1984) has written a comprehensive and influential piece on product quality that explains the lack of agreement as stemming from differences in the disciplinary vantage points of those treating the subject. The transcendental (*philosophic*) view holds quality to be an indefinable, innate property of the product, recognized only through experience. The product-based (*economic*) claim that quality can be measured precisely in terms of some attribute(s) of the product; e.g. a high quality hamburger weighs more and has higher fat content. Garvin notes that product durability is often a measure of quality in high volume consumer goods: "the longer the service life of the item, the higher is its quality."

9.2.2 The Answer Resides with the User

The user-based view, where "quality lies in the eyes of the beholder," conforms with the Total Quality Management (TQM) perspective of agent-based assessment. Quality is demonstrated by the product that best meets the user's need. The concern for quality became a major driving force in changes of management roles in the 1980s. The philosophy, teachings and techniques of W. Edwards Deming, J.M. Juran, and others that took on the TQM label were seen as transforming Japan into an international economic power. The roots of TQM are found in statistical quality control dating to the early work of Shewhart (1931, 1939). The concepts became widely recognized in the 1970s, but their application in Japanese consumer-oriented manufacturing enterprises stretches back into the 1950s. Extension of certain concepts to service industries and more "build-to-contract" products came later, and the evolution can be partially traced in Deming's classic, *Out of the Crisis*, published in 1986. The TQM label is attributed to the US Navy, and books on TQM and variations (e.g. the Taguchi Method) appeared in the mid-1980s. Publications explicitly addressing TQM applied to software lagged by about ten years.

This user-based perspective seems quite reasonable on the surface, but more in-depth analysis provokes two troubling questions:

1. If Product A meets user needs to a greater degree than Product B, it is certainly *preferable*, but is it *better* (of higher quality)?

2. What truly reflects quality when multiple users judge their needs as being different, or being markedly different in importance?

9.2.3 The Producer Has the Answer

The manufacturing-based view is that quality is "conformance to requirements." Deviations from requirements reflect a loss of quality. This is an engineering and producer's view, leading to an equivalence of quality with *product reliability*. The end goal is cost reduction: improvements in quality lead to fewer defects thus causing less rework. This view is clear in a mid-1930s characterization of quality. The description of quality, taken from the foundry industry, is that the product is free of defects. Eleven causes of casting defects, are categorized (e.g. sand holes, scabs and swells), and the cure for each is identified (Roe and Lytle, 1935, p. 99).

A mid-1950s view, taken from a broader industrial context, is that quality to a manufacturer is making "the best product he can *for the price that he can get*" (emphasis as shown in the source) (Moore, 1958, p. 652). The author of this widely used text in industrial engineering and management courses states that ". . . as a rule, the higher the quality, the higher the cost. Worse, even, costs go up faster than quality. A little more quality costs a good bit more money." An important step in product design is the specification of tolerances – the deviations from perfection. Assurance that the product is within tolerance is accomplished by *inspection*.

The purpose of inspection is preventive – not remedial according to Moore (1958, p. 653). By catching the bad product through inspection, no further effort is expended on an unacceptable item, and the reasons for bad (out-of-tolerance) pieces can be identified and the problems corrected. The focus is clearly on *product*. Quality standards come from drawings and written specifications that "describe *what the product should be like* after it is made rather than *how to make it*" (emphasis as given in the source). Quality is meeting the tolerances for dimensional characteristics or conformance with specifications for color, texture, or test results.

The industrial example from the mid-1950s falls into the *value-based* definition suggested by Garvin. He cites Broh (1982, p. 8) who states that "quality is the degree of excellence at an acceptable price and the control of variability at an acceptable cost." A high quality product conforms to requirements and meets an acceptable production cost. Garvin (1984, p. 28) notes that the difficulty in implementing an approach to quality assessment stems from the "blending of two related but distinct concepts:" quality – a reflector of excellence, and value – a measure of worth. The result is "affordable excellence," a somewhat confused and confusing characterization that is difficult to apply.

9.2.4 Answers Lack Temporal Persistence

Further complicating the understanding of quality is the shifting in the importance of product attributes in goods and services that occurs over time. For example, Garvin notes that product durability is often cited as a measure of quality. However, he explains that equating durability with quality is a relatively recent (late nineteenth century) perception ushered in by industrial mass production of consumer goods (Garvin 1984, p. 27). Prior to that time delicate goods, requiring frequent repair or replacement, were affordable only by the wealthy, who certainly demanded "the highest quality."

The transitory nature of a general understanding of the meaning is found in the widespread acceptance of quality as an objective constrained by manufacturing cost in the foundry example above. This view, so well accepted in the 1970s, is completely shoved aside by the rush to embrace TQM by a 1980s consumer population frustrated and even angered by years of shoddy products and services. Crosby (1979) takes an even more contradictory position by arguing that imposing higher quality actually accomplishes a reduction in cost through the elimination of re-work.

9.3 What about Software?

On top of this disconcerting if not confusing backdrop of views of quality in general comes the complicating factor that software production is mentally intensive, quite unlike the physical and mechanical processes implicitly assumed above. This distinction while significant does not alter the characterization of quality in software as much as does the type of software being produced. Several tenets cited above pertain to software as we note in the following section.

9.3.1 Types of Software

Software can be categorized in several ways, e.g. systems versus applications or interactive versus batch, but from the quality perspective the differentiation most significant is "shrink-wrapped" versus "custom development." Shrink-wrapped software is software that is developed by a vendor with the objective of high volume sales. The components of Microsoft Office™ are an obvious example. Software produced under custom development is generally intended for a restricted set of customers according to contracted requirements within a formal project organization.

While shrink-wrapped software can be developed within a project framework, the schedule, conduct of reviews, binding of personnel, and stringency of reporting responsibility are generally less exacting, which explains the use of the term "formal." Requirements are set by a unit of the vendor organization and can be changed without variations being subject to contract conditions. The intended customer community is amorphous, which has both positive and negative implications. Lacking a physical manifestation of the customer, individuals or organizations, the developing group is not tied to satisfying specific needs or hearing reactive complaints. On the other hand, if the final result misses an unrecognized target by too much, the sales could also miss a targeted level with ominous consequences.

An accepted if not mandatory practice with custom developed software is to make frequent interaction with the customer part of the contract specifications. Note that the term "customer" is not necessarily synonymous with "user." In many US government agencies an acquisition office oversees the development of software intended for a separate user community with support during deployment provided by yet a third organization referred to as the In-service Engineering Support Agent. In this case, three customers, only one of which is "the user," have very different interests, responsibilities and sensitivities. Who makes the decision on quality acceptance, or how is a consensus reached? How should a quality measurement program be structured to meet these differences?

9.3.2 Product and Process

The assertion that the key to creation of a high quality product is the production process seems almost trite; yet the early history of software quality assessment reveals a focus on code metrics almost to the exclusion of the activities underlying the creation of code and documentation. The predilection for code metrics obviously stems from the ease with which automated analysis can be applied. However, just as obvious is the realization that little correction can be applied to quality shortcomings recognized in code – at least for the current product.

Process measurement is manual, demanding and expensive. Moreover, while code and documentation measurement is immature, process quality is infantile in comparison. The decades of application of techniques in statistical quality control to industrial production suggest that process monitoring is the key to quality improvement. Quality control charts that detect systematic deviations from quality targets allow corrective actions to be taken before the deviations are unacceptable. Non-systematic but recurring variations beyond acceptable levels can be investigated for underlying causes rather than be left as problems for discovery by the user. A total approach to software quality management requires process, documentation and code measurement. Assessment techniques should be followed by corrective actions, and the problem areas should be re-examined in a mandatory follow-up. A formal audit procedure is highly recommended for large organizations.

9.4 The Evolving Views of Software Quality

Sources on software quality take widely varying approaches in defining the subject. Early views draw a "rough" equivalence between software quality and the number of faults or defects. This perception might be traceable to the strong influence of Shewhart on statistical methods for control of product quality. Since these are roots shared with the Deming philosophy and the TQM movement, a "manufacturing flavor" is detectable. Yet, Shewhart shows remarkable insight in recognizing the linkages that contribute to the difficulty in defining quality (Shewhart 1931, Chapter 4):

> The difficulty in defining quality is to translate future needs of the user into measurable characteristics, so that a product can be designed and turned out to give satisfaction at a price that the user will pay. This is not easy, and as soon as one feels fairly successful in the endeavor, he finds that the needs of the consumer have changed, competitors have moved in, there are new materials to work with, some better than the old ones, some worse; some cheaper than the old ones, some dearer.

Other authors, for example Burr and Owen (1996), base their approach strictly on statistical quality control (or statistical process control). They express the definition of quality in the targeted goal of software with "zero defects." Recognizing that achievement of such a goal is not realistic, they suggest that an a priori acceptable defect level be defined as "the quality of the software" (Burr and Owen, 1996, p. xvi). An implicit equivalence of quality with number and/or severity of defects is found in the **ami** (applications of **m**easurement in **i**ndustry) project (Pulford *et al.* 1996). Colson and Prell (1992) adopt a TQM view emphasizing process management but imply that the meaning of software quality is organizationally defined.

A number of sources (Arthur, 1993; Dunn, 1990; Hetzel, 1993; Fenton and Pfleeger, 1997) choose not to define the term and proceed to describe measures for its determination. For example, Ashley (1995, p. 136) declines to provide a definition with the explanation that "the quality of a software system has many contributing factors, and it is not meaningful to try to encapsulate them into a single subjective definition." Clapp and Stanton (1992) intertwine the definition with the goal of measurement by claiming that "software quality is a set of measurable characteristics that satisfies the buyers, users and maintainers of a software product." Gillies (1992, pp. 12–15) notes several definitions in describing the multiple dimensions of quality and cites Garvin's five views. He concludes with the "sound byte" assertion that "Quality is people."

Several authors cite the International Organization of Standardization (ISO) standard (ISO 8402–1994, p.6), which defines software quality as "the totality of features and characteristics of a product or service that bear on its ability to meet stated or implied needs." This view is expressed even earlier by Tausworthe (1977, p. 56) who identifies the features as reliability, maintainability, modifiability, generality, usability, and performance. The definitions expressed in the standard and by Tausworthe are similar to that adopted by OPA.

A particularly instructive view is offered by Musa et al. (1987, p. 5), who state that "three of the most important software product characteristics are quality, cost, and schedule." They go on to say:

Quantitative measures exist for the latter two characteristics, but the quantification of quality has been more difficult. It is most important, however, because the absence of a concrete measure for software quality means that quality will suffer when it competes for attention against cost and schedule. In fact, this absence may be the principal reason for the well known existence of quality problems in many software products.

In closing this capsulated trace of software evolution, the lack of universal acceptance of a meaning for "software quality" must be admitted. However, convergence on several key points seems clear.

- Quality is not revealed simply by the absence of defects; rather, software must exhibit several component characteristics to be considered "high quality."

- Quality must be judged from a customer perspective, but complex software systems can have "customers" with widely differing priorities on components of quality (acquisition agent, in-service support organization, user).

- Product quality cannot endure and improve without an organizational commitment to the advancement of process quality.

- The measurement of software quality must be comprehensive, involving process artifacts and events, documentation (beyond just deliverables) and code.

- Automated measurement is required for code assessment, but the results allow only limited correction for *the current product.*

- Process measurement of quality is manually intensive but the predictive use of results enables adjustments to improve quality in *the current product.*

- No single measure of software quality is possible or useful.

Reflection on these key points serves as a guide to the rationale leading to development of the OPA Framework for measuring and managing software quality.

9.5 Software Quality: A Standards View

Standards exist for many, if not all, aspects of the software and systems evolution. The International Organization for Standardization (ISO) is the principal actor on the world scene (http://www.iso.ch/iso/en/ISOOnline.frontpage, accessed on 1 December 2001). The ISO 9000 family of standards applies to quality in a broad sense with ISO 9000: 2000 providing vocabulary and foundational material and ISO 9001 defining the requirements for quality management. Most of the remainder of the family are presented as guidelines. This is the case for ISO 10012 which deals with measurement. Within the ISO, standards are developed by Technical Committees with representatives from participating national standards development bodies. These national bodies also develop standards. The dominant UK body is the British Standards Institution (BSI) (http//www.bsi-global.com/index.html, last accessed on 5 December 2001). The USA has both the American National Standards Institute (ANSI) (http://www.ansi.org, last accessed on 5th December 2001) and the Institute for Electrical and Electronic Engineers (IEEE). Within the latter organization the IEEE Computer Society has responsibility for software-related standards, which is managed by the Software Engineering Standards Committee (SESC) (http://www.computer.org/standards/sesc/, last accessed on 5 December 2001).

The role of standardization in software engineering is complex and sometimes controversial. A cynical view that often goes unexpressed is that the time to standardize is when no one cares. The rationale behind this view is that premature standardization hinders innovation and technical development. When the best practices and proper techniques are widely acknowledged and accepted, standards are unnecessary. A more realistic and pragmatic perspective is that standards are necessary to promote the adoption and success of technology, but standards should evolve to reflect progress in scientific understanding and the consequent technological change. An evolutionary and adaptive strategy for standards development is characteristic of the organizations cited above, and on-line access promotes currency in the use of standards.

Knowledge of measurement standards is essential in setting up a program if customers require conformance with specific product standards on deliverables. The complexity in understanding the role of each measurement standard and the relationships among them is beyond the scope of this book. An excellent scource that is reasonably current as this book goes to press is (Moore, 1998).

References

ADAR (1995) Ada 95 Rationale – The Language – The Standard Libraries, International Standard ISO/IEC–8652:1995. Intermetrics, Inc, Cambridge, MA

Arthur JD and Nance RE (1987) Developing an automated procedure for evaluating software development methodologies and associated products. Technical report SRC-87–007, Department of Computer Science and Systems Research Center. Virginia Tech, Blacksburg, VA

Arthur JD and Nance RE (1990) A framework for assessing the adequacy and effectiveness of software development methodologies. In: Proceedings of the Fifteenth Annual Software Engineering Workshop, Process Improvement Session. Greenbelt, MD

Arthur JD, Nance RE, Bundy GN, Dorsey EV and Henry J (1991) Software quality measurement: validation of a foundational approach. Technical report SRC–91–002, Systems Research Center and Department of Computer Science. Virginia Tech, Blacksburg, VA

Arthur LJ (1985) Measuring programmer productivity and software quality. John Wiley, New York

Arthur LJ (1993) Improving software quality: an insider's guide to TQM. John Wiley, New York

Ashley N (1995) Measurement as a powerful software management tool. McGraw-Hill Book Company Europe, Berkshire

Balci O (1994) Validation, verification, and testing techniques throughout the life-cycle of a simulation study. Annals of Operations Research, 53:121–173

Basili VR and Weiss DM (1985) A methodology for collecting valid software engineering data. IEEE Transactions on Software Engineering, 11:2:157–168

Basili VR and Rombach HD (1988) The TAME Project: towards improvement-oriented software environments. IEEE Transactions on Software Engineering. 14:6:759–773

Boehm BW (1988) A spiral model of software development and enhancement. IEEE Computer, 21:5:61–72

Booch G (1983) Software components with Ada. The Benjamin/Cummings Publishing Company, Menlo Park, CA

Booch G (1987) Software components with Ada. The Benjamin/Cummings Publishing Company, Menlo Park, CA

Broh RA (1982) Managing Quality for Higher Projects, McGraw-Hill, Inc., New York

Bundy GN (1990) Assessing software quality in Ada-based products with the objectives, principles attributes framework. Master's thesis, Department of Computer Science. Virginia Tech, Blacksburg, VA

Burr A and Owen M (1996) Statistical Methods for Software Quality: Using Metrics to Control Process and Product Quality. International Thomson Computer Press, New York, NY

Carmines EG and Zeller RA (1979) Reliability and Validity Assessment, Quantitative Applications in the Social Sciences, JL Sullivan (ed.). Sage Publications, Beverly Hills, CA

Carley M (1981) Social Measurement and Social Indicators. George Allen and Unwin, Boston, MA

Clapp JA and Stanton SF (1992) A guide to total software quality control, RL–TR–92–316, vol 1, December. Rome Laboratory, Air Force Material Command, Griffiss Air Force Base, New York

Colson JS Jr and Prell EM (1992) Total quality management for a large software project. AT&T Technical Journal, May–June, 48–56

Conway RD, Gries D and Zimmerman E (1976) A Primer on Pascal. Winthrop Computer Systems Series, Cambridge, MA

Crosby PB (1979) Quality is Free: The Art of Making Quality Certain, McGraw-Hill, Inc., New York

Dale N and Orshalick D (1983) Introduction to Pascal and standard design. D.C. Heath & Company, Lexington, MA

Dandekar AV (1987) A procedural approach to the evaluation of software development methodologies. Master's thesis, Department of Computer Science, Virginia Tech, Blacksburg, VA

Deming WE (1986) Out of Crisis, Massachusetts Institute of Technology, Center for Advannced Engineering Study, Cambridge, MA

Dorsey EV (1992) The automated assessment of computer software documentation quality using the Objectives/Principles/Attributes framework. Master's thesis, Department of Computer Science, Virginia Tech, Blacksburg, VA.

Dunn RH (1990) Software quality: concepts and plans. Prentice-Hall, Inc, Englewood Cliffs, NJ

Dunsmore HE and Gannon JD (1980) Analysis of the effects of programming factors on programming effort. Journal of Systems and Software, 1:2:1044–1050

Ejiogu LO (1987) The critical issues of software metrics – Part 0. Perspectives on software measurements. SIGPLAN Notices, 22:3:59–64

Elmendorf DC (May/June 1992) Managing Quality and Quality Improvement. AT&T Technical Journal; 57–65

Embley DW and Woodfield SN (1988) Assessing the quality of abstract data types written in Ada. In: Proceedings: 10th International Conference on Software Engineering, 144–153

Fenton NE and Pfleeger SL (1997) Software Metrics: A Rigorous and Practical Approach, 2nd edn. Thomson Computer Press,Boston, MA

Florac WA, Park RE and Carleton AD(1997) Practical software measurement: measuring for process management and improvement, Guidebook CMU/SEI-97-HB-003, April 1997

Gaffney J and Cruickshank R (1980) Indicators for software design assessment. IBM FSD Final Report on Creative Development, Task 91

Gannon JD, Katz EE and Basili VR (1986) Metrics for Ada packages: an initial study. Communications of the ACM, 29:7:616–623

Garvin DA (Fall 1984) What does "product quality" really mean? In: Product quality. Harvard Business Review, 25–45

Ghezzi C and Jazayeri M (1982) Programming Language Concepts. John Wiley & Sons, Inc, New York

Giddings RV (1984) Accommodating uncertainty in software design. Comm. ACM, 27:5:428–434

Gillies AC (1992) Software quality: theory and management. Chapman & Hall, New York, NY

Glass RL (1992) Building quality software. Prentice Hall, Englewood Cliffs, NJ

Halstead MH (1977) Elements of software science. Elsevier North-Holland, Inc, New York

Henry S and Kafura D (1981) Software structure metrics based on information flow. IEEE Transactions on Software Engineering, 7:5:510–518

Hetzel B (1993) Making Software Measurement Work: Building an Effective Measurement Program. QED Publishing Group, P.O. Box 812070, Wellesley, MA 02181–0013

Humphrey WS 1990. Managing the Software Process. SEI Series in Software Engineering, Addison-Wesley, Reading, MA

ISO 8042 (1994) Quality Management and Quality Assurance – Vocabulary, International Organization for Standardization, ISO TC176 Collection, Geneva, Switzerland

Kearney JK, Sedlmeyer RL, Thompson WB, Grey MA and Adler MA (1986) Software complexity measurement. Communications of the ACM 29, 11:1044–1050

Lavender RG (1988) The explication of process-product relationships in DoD-STD-2167 and DoD-STD-2168 via an augmented data flow diagram model. Master's thesis, Department of Computer Science, Virginia Tech, Blacksburg, VA

Lehman MM (1984) A Further Model of Coherent Programming Processes, in Proceedings of the Software Process Workshop, IEEE Computer Society Press, Piscataway, NY, pp. 27–35

Marca D (1984) Applying Software Engineering Principles. Little, Brown and Company, Boston, MA

McCabe TJ (1976) A complexity measure. IEEE Transactions on Software Engineering, 2:4:308–320

McCall JA, Richards PK and Walters GF (1977) Factors in software quality. Technical report RADC-TR-77–369, Rome Air Defense Center, Rome, NY

Meier K and Brudney J (1981) Applied Statistics for Public Administration. Duxbury Press, Boston, MA

Moore FG (1958) Manufacturing Management, Revised Edition. Richard D Irwin, Inc., Homeward, IL

Moore JW (1998) Software Engineering Standards: A User's Road Map, IEEE Computer Society Press, Los Alamitos, CA

Musa JDm Iannino A and Okumoto K (1987) Software reliability: measurement, prediction, application. McGraw-Hill Book Company

Nance RE and Arthur JD (1994) Software quality measurement: Assessment, prediction, and validation. Technical report SRC–94–006, Systems Research Center and Department of Computer Science, Virginia Tech, Blacksburg, VA

Nance RE and Arthur RD (1994) Software quality measurement : assessment, prediction and validation. The Sixth Annual Software Technology Conference, Track 2: Software Testing, Measurement and Inspection. Salt Lake City, UT

Nance RE, Arthur JD and Dandekar AV (1986) Evaluation of software development methodologies. Technical report SRC–86–010, Systems Research Center and Department of Computer Science, Virginia Tech, Blacksburg, VA

Pulford K, Kutzmann-Combelles A and Shirlaw S (1996) A Quantitative Approach to Software Management: The Ami Handbook. Addison-Wesley, Reading, MA

Rose JW and Lytle CW (1935) Factory Equipment, First Edition. International Textbook Company, Scranton, PA. Copyright in Great Britain

Ross DL (1986) Classifying Ada packages. Ada Letters, 6:4:53–65

Sanders J and Curran E (1994) Software Quality: A Framework for Success in Software Development and Support. Addison-Wesley Publishing Co, Reading, MA

Shewhart WA (1931) Economic control of quality of manufactured product. Van Nostrand, New York (American Society of Quality Control, 1980, reprinted by Ciepress, The George Washington University, 1986), 473–491

Shewhart WA (1939) Statistical method from the viewpoint of quality control by Walter A Shewhart . . . with the editorial assistance of W Edwards Deming. The Graduate School, The Department of Agriculture, WA

Stevens WP (1981) Using structured design. John Wiley & Sons, Inc, New York

Stevens WP, Myers GJ and Constantine LL (1994) Structured design. IBM Systems Journal, 13:2:115–139

Swanson EB (1976) The dimensions of maintenance. Proceedings of the Second International Conference on Software Engineering, 492–497

Tasuworthe RC (1977) Standardized Development of Computer Software. Prentice Hall, Inc, Englewood Cliffs, NJ

Troy DA and Zweben SH (1981) Measuring the quality of structured design. Journal of Systems and Software; 4:2:113–120

Wichmann BA (1984a) Is Ada too big? A designer answers the critics. Communications of the ACM, 27:2:98–103

Wichmann BA (1984b) A comparison of Pascal and Ada. In: comparing and assessing Programming Languages. Prentice-Hall, Inc, Englewood Cliffs, NJ

Yourdon E and Constantine LL (1978) Structured design. Yourdon, Inc, New York

Zage WM, Zage DM and Wilburn C (1995) Avoiding metric monsters: A design metric approach. Annals of Software Engineering, 1:43–56

Index

PRACTITIONER SERIES

Series Editor: **Ray Paul**
Editorial Board: **Frank Bott, Nic Holt,**
Kay Hughes, Elizabeth Hull,
Richard Nance, Russel Winder and Sion Wyn

These books are written
by practitioners for practitioners.

They offer thoroughly practical hands-on advice on how to tackle specific problems. So, if you are already a practitioner in the development, exploitation or management of IS/IT systems, or you need to acquire an awareness and knowledge of principles and current practice in an IT/IS topic fast then these are the books for you.

All books in this series will be clear, concise and problem solving and will cover a wide range of areas including:
- systems design techniques
- performance modelling
- cost and estimation control
- software maintenance
- quality assurance
- database design and administration
- HCI
- safety critical systems
- distributed computer systems
- internet and web applications
- communications, networks and security
- multimedia, hypermedia and digital libraries
- object technology
- client-server
- formal methods
- design approaches
- IT management

All books are, of course, available from all good booksellers (who can order them even if they are not in stock), but if you have difficulties you can contact the publishers direct, by telephoning +44 (0) 1483 418822 (in the UK & Europe), +1/212/4 60/15 00 (in the USA), or by emailing orders@svl.co.uk

www.springer.de   www.springer-ny.com